DIVORCE?

Facing the Issues of Marital Breakdown

Edited by Mags O'Brien

Basement Press
DUBLIN

First published in Ireland in 1995 by
Basement Press
an imprint of Attic Press Ltd
29 Upper Mount Street
Dublin 2

A catalogue record for this title is available from the British Library

ISBN 1 85594 195 3

The moral right of Mags O'Brien and the individual authors has been asserted.

Cover design and typesetting: Verbatim Typesetting & Design.
Printing: The Guernsey Press Co. Ltd

This book is published with the financial assistance of the Arts Council/An Comhairle Ealaíon, Ireland

Obviou
time and patience of those named who contributed chapters and whose thoughtful work is much appreciated. Thanks are also due to Ita Mangan, Róisín McDermott, Maura Wall-Murphy and Ita O'Connor, who gave of their time and expertise; groups such as AIM, Contact, Parents Alone and the Separated Persons Association, as well as to the members of the various religious denominations who contributed, with unfailing courtesy. Mary Buckley from the NCIR library for references; Tracey Leahy, Paul Daly and Cale Teager from the DAG office, who gave invaluable assistance with the information section and the laborious task of input and correction. Thanks are also due to all those in Basement Press involved in the publication of this book, for their patience, and to members and staff of DAG past and present who gave assistance, including Marie Maher, Mary O'Hagan and Anne O'Brien. Thanks also to Niall Courtenay for answering my many 'what if' questions. Finally to Jack McGinley; without his encouragement and unfailing support there would have been no book.

Mags O'Brien
February 1995

Dedication

In affectionate memory of Phyllis McGhee, Joe O'Connor and Heather Aylward, whose tenacity and humour will be sadly missed on the campaign trail.

Contents

Introduction

There will undoubtedly be calls for a 'civilised' debate in the lead-up to the next referendum on divorce. It seems inevitable, however, that temperatures will be raised on both sides because on the one hand, the issue affects the very fabric of peoples' lives on a personal scale, and on the other, it is seen as a threat to the old order.

In 1986 opponents argued that divorce actually causes marital breakdown. It has become increasingly clear that, in our Irish 'divorce-free zone', marriages are breaking down at an ever-increasing rate. From 1986 to 1991 marital-breakdown figures showed a staggering increase of 48 per cent, or over 3,500 per year (census figures). This illustrates that the legal process of divorce, which is the final chapter in the demise of a marriage, cannot be blamed for the preceding breakdown. It should also be increasingly obvious that referenda are unsuitable methods of dealing with social problems, as defeat cannot be viewed as a solution to the problems addressed. Unfortunately, the Constitution of 1937, which casts a long shadow, means that they are presently the only mechanism available to us.

In 1986, opinion polls showed that a comfortable majority supported divorce in certain circumstances. The pendulum quickly swung the other way, culminating in defeat for the pro-divorce lobby: a result which caused much anguish and bitterness. It was inevitable that those who supported the introduction of divorce and, more especially, those of us who sought a solution to our own legal limbo, should feel thus. It seemed that our calls for compassion had been ignored and that friends and, sometimes, families had denied us a second chance. In hindsight it is easier to see that voters had eventually become punch-drunk with claims and counter-claims, threats of eternal damnation, statistic-slinging and 'expert' quoting by both sides. If members of the government were unable to explain the intricacies surrounding the implementation of the legislation, it is entirely understandable that those not personally affected by marital breakdown should hesitate to introduce a measure which had been so demonised.

This book has been compiled in an effort to discuss the complex legal, financial, social and psychological problems that marital breakdown brings. While the project was started at least two years before the time of writing, it has taken on a life of its own, with several rewrites of entire chapters in an effort to keep up with the dizzying pace of changes that have taken place. (The nine years since the last referendum have seen more reforms in family law than the fifty-eight years since the enactment of the 1937 Constitution.) It seems that, although the 1986 pro-divorce campaign failed, it served to heighten public awareness of the problems faced by separated people, and put the issue firmly on the political agenda, where it will stay until solutions are found.

As this book goes to press there are still more reforms in the pipeline. It would be impossible continually to re-edit to keep pace with these changes; therefore what has been attempted is to update the research and thinking in the areas covered to reflect the position at the beginning of 1995.

There is also a practical aspect to this book, which aims to give information on services available to those who have recently separated. Each of the writers has contributed from her or his own area of expertise; therefore, there may be differences in viewpoints or interpretations. Such differences are healthy and can only aid the forthcoming debate.

The History of Divorce in Ireland

including the 1986 referendum and subsequent changes

Mags O'Brien

Until the ninth century, divorce by mutual consent was available in Ireland for those whose marriage had broken down. Historians feel that the legal framework which included the provision for divorce was brought to Ireland by early missionaries. Women were permitted to divorce their husbands for a variety of reasons, including wife-beating, sterility and failure to pay maintenance; men could obtain a divorce because of their wife's infidelity, infertility or bad management. (MacCurtain, 1978) These provisions were adapted into the first recorded Irish legal system, Brehon law.

From the twelfth century onwards, the Roman Catholic Church in Europe, having previously permitted divorce, began to insist that marriage was an indissoluble bond. Such an idea was strongly resisted by the Irish, who viewed marriage as a private arrangement between two people, and one which should not be interfered with by the Church.

After the Norman invasion there was a gradual integration of English common law into the Irish system. Common law also permitted the dissolution of marriage. However, the late nineteenth century saw an increase in conservatism in Ireland, and though the laws relating to divorce were liberalised in England, Irish legislation remained unaltered. Under the 1857 Divorce Act, divorce was still permissible, but only through individual applications to Westminster. This right to grant divorces was not automatically passed to the Dáil after Independence and the first Constitution of 1922. Between 1912 and 1937, three Private Members Bills were introduced in an attempt to bring Irish divorce legislation up to date. (Divorce Action Group, 1985.) It was on the 1925 Private Members Bill that William Butler Yeats made his most notable contribution in the Senate. (Tuohy, 1976:188)

Yeats knew well that divorce would not be permitted in the Free State, but he made the political point that such a Bill

9

would drive a wedge between the North and South and make partition irreversible: '...I think it tragic that within three years of this country gaining its independence we should be discussing a measure which a minority of this nation considers to be grossly oppressive. I am proud to consider myself a typical man of that minority. We against whom you have done this thing are no petty people. We are one of the great stocks of Europe. We are the people of Burke; we are the people of Grattan; we are the people of Swift, the people of Emmet, the people of Parnell. We have created the most modern literature of this country. We have created the best of its political intelligence.'

While Touhy asserts that this speech reflects Yeats's own particular sectarianism, it in no way detracts from the fact that the Protestant minority felt alienated by the influence of Rome on the new state.

THE 1937 CONSTITUTION
The strong Catholic ethos pervading Irish life and influencing its laws was substantially a result of the continued domination of Ireland by Britain. Basil Chubb, writing on the politics of the Irish Constitution, cites David Martin on nationalism and secularisation:

an indissoluble union of church and nation arises in those situations where the church has been the sole available vehicle of nationality against foreign domination: Greece, Cyprus, Poland, Belgium, Ireland, Croatia...The countries mentioned remain areas of high practice and belief...The myth of identity is strengthened further when the dominant group have been at the border with another faith.

This rigid adherence to religion is evident in Bunreacht na hEireann, the Irish Constitution of 1937. While this was the brainchild of Eamon de Valera (who submitted it to the Pope for approval), its articles on social policy were a reflection of the thinking of the vast majority of the population at that time. A significant amount of opposition to the Constitution came from women's groups, who were alarmed by provisions relating to the family. These provisions purported to give women special recognition and protection, but actually reduced their rights as individuals.

The Constitution was narrowly passed (by 51 per cent) and includes Article 41.3.2, which prohibits divorce, as follows:

No law shall be enacted providing for the grant of a dissolution of marriage.

W T Cosgrave, although accepting the rights of the Church as arbiter of 'moral' values, complained about the Constitutional provisions against divorce, as he felt that these negated his guarantee of minority rights. He quickly became the victim of a smear campaign and was accused of falling under the influence of the Freemasons.

The Catholic Bulletin stated, of the minorities:

Let them, if they so wish, set up their own divorce courts. That they should call on Catholic voters to do evil in God's sight, by setting up a divorce mill, is intolerable insolence. (*Irish Times:* 1986)

In 1967, Seán Lemass established an All Party Committee on the Constitution which, under George Colley's chairmanship, concluded that divorce should be available for those who married in a religion that allowed it. Archbishop John McQuaid retorted that 'If anyone were allowed divorce, everyone would want it.'

The proposal was dropped immediately.

In the continuing debate on the unification of Ireland, an interesting idea was put forward by Charles J. Haughey – the inventor of Irish solutions to Irish problems – that in a united Ireland there might be different practices for different regions! (*Irish Times*: 1986)

Of course the 1937 ban on divorce did not mean that marital breakdown was non-existent in Ireland, but the resulting social stigma of a failed marriage meant that many couples kept their situation secret. Often men went abroad to work and form second relationships, while other couples remained in the same home but had no communication. Precise figures are not available, because the census did not then include a category for separated people, but in the 1979 census 7,624 people admitted to a status other than married, single or widowed. By 1981 this figure had increased to 14,117.

THE FORMATION OF THE DIVORCE ACTION GROUP

In 1980 a group of women in Coolock got together with the objective of campaigning for the removal of the Constitutional ban on divorce. For such a change to be made to the Constitution, a referendum must be put to the people and passed by a simple majority. This meeting in Coolock led to the creation of Divorce Action Group (DAG). From its formation DAG lobbied politicians and attempted to highlight the problems encountered by those in marital-breakdown situations and in second relationships.

Membership of the group increased rapidly; mainly made up of separated people, it also included political activists, who saw divorce as a civil-rights issue. DAG also fulfilled a dual role; many members used it as a support group as well as an action group.

THE 1980S

After Ireland's entry to the European Community, there was speculation that various articles of the Irish Constitution, including the ban on divorce, might run counter to EC legislation and could be challenged in the European courts. On the question of divorce it was felt that, while the Irish Constitution recognised only the family based on marriage, the European Convention on Human Rights gave rights to 'a second family who actually live together in a family relationship'. A test case was brought to Europe by Roy Johnston, who was represented by Mary Robinson SC. Sadly, the final ruling of the Commission argued that Article 12 of the Convention, which recognises the right to marry and found a family, did not expressly recognise the right to remarry. The European Convention, while based on the International Bill of Human Rights, does not specifically state that there is a human right to dissolution of marriage. The court did, however, find that the child of this second relationship had been discriminated against, and therefore the Irish Government was forced to introduce the Status of Children Act, which virtually abolished the concept of illegitimacy in Ireland.

By July 1983, the increased number of separations in the Republic had prompted the government to set up the Joint Oireachtas Committee on Marital Breakdown. The Committee's conclusions were that a referendum should be held, and that any such referendum 'should be in a positive format, replacing the present article 41.3.2 with a provision specifically authorising the Oireachtas to legislate for the dissolution of marriage'.

The Fianna Fáil members of the Committee objected to the recommendations for the introduction of divorce but were out-voted.

The report of the Committee fuelled the ongoing divorce debate as it served to highlight the increase in breakdowns. In the wake of the Joint Oireachtas Committee and the Johnston ruling, Michael O'Leary, TD introduced a further unsuccessful Private Member's Bill on divorce.

1986 REFERENDUM

On 24 April 1986, the coalition government of Fine Gael and Labour called a referendum to be held on 26 June, for an addition to article 41.3.2.

Section 3.1 reads as follows:

The state pledges itself to guard with special care the institution of marriage, on witch the family is founded, and to protect it against attack.

The proposed Section 3.2 read:

Where, and only where, such court established under this constitution as may be prescribed by law is satisfied that a marriage has failed, the failure has continued for a period of, or periods amounting to, at least five years, there is no reasonable possibility of reconciliation between the parties to the marriage, and any other condition prescribed by law has been complied with, the court may in accordance with law grant a dissolution of the marriage provided that the court is satisfied that adequate and proper provision having regard to the circumstances will be made for any dependent spouse and for any child of or any child who is dependent on either spouse.

While DAG had been actively campaigning, they had not envisaged a referendum for at least another year. Its executive (chaired by John O'Connor, as Jean Tansey was out of the country) met on the evening of the announcement and, while the consensus was that a five-year time frame was excessive, decided to support the legislation because they felt that members would welcome any chance of divorce. They also hoped that the public might be less likely to reject such a restrictive regime.

In his autobiography, Garrett FitzGerald states that he called the referendum in 1986 because opinion polls were showing that a favourable outcome was likely and because he wanted the issue of divorce off the agenda before 1987, when a general election was due. He felt that if the referendum were not held in 1986, the Government would have been attacked both by liberals for not having called a referendum and by Fianna Fáil for intending to introduce divorce on demand.

Although opinion polls had indeed been encouraging, it became clear from the first week of the campaign that more groundwork was needed from the Government if the referendum were to be carried. While social commentators have ventured many opinions as to the cause of the massive turnaround in public opinion (63.1 per cent voting against was the final outcome), the main reason for the defeat was the lack of legislation to underpin the amendment. Worries about property, maintenance and deserted wives' allowances were major factors, and were seized on by the anti-divorce campaigners. Margaret Fine Davis (1988) found that while the Catholic view of marriage as a lifelong commitment played an important part in the eventual outcome, such 'attitudes were closely tied into issues concerning the economic and social consequences of divorce for the wife'.

GOVERNMENT DISARRAY

During the run-up to the referendum, the government's attitude was incoherent at best, with many of the most vociferous anti-divorce campaigners coming from within the Fine Gael ranks. Perhaps the most notable were Alice Glenn TD (remembered mainly for her assertion that women voting for divorce were like turkeys voting for Christmas) and Pat Cooney, the Minister for Education.

According to FitzGerald, there had been an agreement in Fine Gael that deputies did not have to positively campaign for the amendment if they were anti-divorce, on the understanding that they would not actually oppose the referendum. However, there appears to have been little real action taken to censure Cooney and others; it seems that FitzGerald feared making martyrs of them. Some Fine Gael activists feel that if he had been more assertive at this time, the defeat may not have been as decisive.

While Labour had a pro-divorce policy, which meant they were less likely openly to break ranks, some of their rural TDs were either ambivalent or remained silent because they feared a backlash in the following election.

Fianna Fáil, while professing to be neutral, made every effort to undermine the campaign, with Padraig Flynn TD talking of divorce being 'like a Frankenstein stalking the land'.

THE ANTI-DIVORCE CAMPAIGN

In May 1986 an Anti-Divorce Campaign (ADC) was set up, headed by John O'Reilly, William Binchy, Senator Des Hanafin, Michael and Mary Lucey, and Bernadette Bonnar. Most of these are rumoured to have connections with organisations such as Opus Dei, Family Solidarity and the Knights of Columbanus. They were also veterans of the 1983 Amendment Campaign, and it was speculated that they received funding from the Moral Majority in the USA.

The ADC purported to support first families, expressing concern for women and children, whom they maintained would suffer all manner of ills were divorce to be introduced. The reality was that many of the members of DAG campaigning for divorce were these very first families that the ADC claimed to be protecting.

Connections with ultra-conservative Catholic groups – whose influence reaches into government, parts of the civil service and the business world – meant that the ADC had money, power and influence. The lack of clear legislation on social issues allowed them to use scare tactics such as telling farmers they would lose their farms on divorce, while telling the same farmers' wives that they would be thrown out of their homes penniless!

The debate became bruising and frustrating, with the ADC disseminating rumours and half-truths on a daily basis. They bombarded the public with statistics from the USA and England, many of which have since been discredited. One notable example is that of Leonore Wietzman (1985), who stated that her research showed that in the United States, women and children suffered a 73 per cent drop in income after divorce. According to Susan Faludi (1992), her figures have since been disproven by Saul Hoffman, who specialises in divorce statistics, and whose findings were corroborated by the USA Census Bureau (they found a 33 per cent drop in the first year of separation). This is not to say that poverty is not a problem, but it does illustrate the selective use of statistics. Of course the much lower divorce figures in Italy, Spain and Northern Ireland were disregarded.

DIVORCE ACTION GROUP

The Divorce Action Group, which was then chaired by Jean Tansey, with Executive members Clare O'Connor, Margaret Geaney, Martin Lohan, Betty Krysanowski, Mags O'Brien, Ann Walsh, Evelyn Hempenstall, Michael O'Halloran, Andrea Bridges, and its Secretary Karen O'Connor, PRO Joe Dennehy and National Organiser, Michael Taft, were constantly put on the defensive, and became bogged down trying to answer the endless stream of allegations from the myriad groups set up by the ADC. In *Masterminds of the Right*, Emily O'Reilly describes the DAG campaign as shambolic. While this comment is under-standable, the reality was that the majority of those involved were separated people looking for a second chance. As she states, these people lacked the political skills that the ADC had learned through the 1983 Amendment campaign, but, more significantly, lacked the massive funds that their opposition used so effectively for advertising. ADC posters appeared targeting different socio-economic areas stating:

We Want Jobs, not Divorce
Divorce Kills Love
God says Vote No

The Family Prayer Movement, one of the many groups that joined the fray, asked of children: 'Would you like your daddy to walk away for ever and leave you an orphan crying in the night?' A leaflet from the The Irish Family League read:

'Taxpayer pays all – Divorce will cost IR£200 million p.a., IR£17 per week extra out of each taxpayer's pocket'.

The ADC sent out a pamphlet to every home in the country, at an approximate printing and postage cost of £60,000. This sum virtually equalled the total funds available to DAG for the full campaign.

While the ADC plotted, the DAG executive were forced to spend precious time organising fundraisers and doing pub collections rather than planning strategy. A review of the minutes of executive meetings show that fundraising was the major topic on the agenda. As the DAG had been founded to campaign for the removal of the ban on divorce, arguably its job was over when the government called the referendum. Sadly, the group was left to fight on alone against some of the most powerful forces in Irish society, namely the Church, Fianna Fáil and the forces of conservatism.

THE GOVERNMENT CAMPAIGN

Although the Labour Party was active in some constituencies, and ministers of both parties spoke on pro-divorce platforms, the failure of the Government to keep its own house in order meant that in many rural areas, DAG, assisted by volunteers from Labour, the Worker's Party, Sinn Fein and the Communist Party of Ireland, were the only ones pounding the pro-divorce campaign trail. Fine Gael and the PDs issued pro-divorce literature but in many areas did little on the ground because of individual TDs' reluctance to offend their more conservative supporters. Coupled with this, many of the TDs who actually supported divorce were unclear about the intricacies of the legislation and frequently scored 'own goals' when confronted by legal opponents such as William Binchy.

THE CHURCH

The Catholic Church also played a pivotal role in the eventual outcome of the referendum, with religious brave enough to speak out in favour being silenced while traditionalists used the pulpit to pound home their message. Many of the public were already worried and confused by the conflicting opinions reflected daily in the media, and such sermons pushed many waiverers firmly into the 'no' camp. The bishops, while proclaiming freedom of conscience, issued missives that left the faithful in no doubt of their views. One particularly cynical contribution was made by Cardinal Ó Fiach who stated, both before and after the campaign, that divorce would have to be permitted in a united Ireland – and yet opposed its introduction during the referendum.

The hierarchy also attempted to suggest that, in place of divorce legislation, church annulments would suffice for deserving cases. Bishop Casey was most influential in this area and was one of the more conservative bishops, despite the populist image he portrayed.

Many separated Catholics were alienated by the Church's attitude, especially when their children were taunted by others after the Bishop's pronouncements. This alienation has since manifested itself in the increased number of families seeking non-denominational education. The role of the post-Vatican II Church was particularly disappointing in this instance, as it failed to differentiate between the role of pastors and of legislators.

RURAL AREAS

The campaign was particularly lonely and bruising for those brave enough to venture out in rural areas. Many were afraid to voice their support because some of the more influential local luminaries were canvassing on the other side and made it clear that liberal views were not welcome in their town, or from their employees.

THE REFERENDUM – 26 JUNE 1986

On the day of the referendum the ADC machine (in some areas, the local Fianna Fáil cumann) mobilised their voters in order to ensure a resounding defeat. Although DAG canvassers realised that support was rapidly waning, they were still unprepared for the astounding swing in public opinion, and were devastated by the result of the vote.

The following morning, as early indications signalled a massive 'No' vote, the DAG headquarters were inundated with triumphalist and abusive calls.

That night many attended a 'wake' in Phyliss and Seán McGhee's house in Leeson Street, Dublin. Volunteers were devastated. It was particularly hard for many to countenance the fact that friends and relations might have voted against giving them freedom. Some subsequently left Ireland, feeling that they could no longer live in a state that denied them basic civil rights. The fact that before the referendum there had been a majority in favour of divorce was a major cause of the bitterness felt by DAG activists, who realised that the vote was not an indication of strongly held moral views but rather of an unwillingness to face change. Their perception was that while many had supported divorce in theory, they wished to preserve their separatist vision of an Ireland somehow more moral and more upright than other nations.

In an article in *Studies* entitled 'Reflections of a Disappointed Pluralist', Father John Brady SJ echoed the feelings of many when he said:

> In the mid-70s there was a sense that Ireland was slowly evolving towards a more tolerant and humane society, more accepting of diversity in beliefs and views on morality, less protective of its citizens, perhaps, and more reliant on a personally adopted code of beliefs and values. In such a society the value of freedom and the value of reconciliation of diverse traditions would be highly developed. Ten years later it is far from clear that this is the way things are going. Irish society, both in its secular and ecclesiastical aspects, has been caught up in the wave of conservatism that swept across the world after 1980. The emphasis is on maintaining things as they were, defending traditional values, fighting off the onset of change. It is hard to detect any serious interest in achieving the pluralist society as a value in its own right, and as something in which Christian values can flourish.

After such a resounding defeat it was remarkable that an opinion poll taken three months earlier and published in the *Irish Independent* showed that over 60 per cent of the population were in favour of divorce under certain circumstances. While campaigners were still bitter, this opinion poll did show that perhaps it was not conservatism that had caused the defeat but rather the fact that waters had been muddied enough during the campaign to disturb a large number of the population.

During the debate, many separated people had gone public

with their stories. DAG's real failure, or perhaps naiveté, was in hoping that the electorate would respond to these pleas for compassion. The opposition, on the other hand, was quite ruthless and pushed the argument away from the plight of individuals to more abstract general concepts. They talked of 'hard cases making bad laws', but did not acknowledge, as Catherine McGuinness SC was later to say, that 'bad laws make hard cases'. The ADC played on the genuine fears of dependent women, glossing over the fact that, in the majority of cases, it is women who actually initiate separations. While the perception was of a 'moral' victory for the anti-divorce camp, the main arguments were really financial.

POST-1986

After the referendum defeat in 1986, it seemed there was a spate of separations; the reality was that many couples who had not admitted that they had separated finally gained the courage to admit it once others were prepared to air their stories. Realising that there was no prospect of a referendum for a number of years, couples also made alternative arrangements, many obtaining foreign divorces. While these are of dubious legality, they do give people a sense of having finished a chapter in their lives and allow them to move on. The majority of these couples remarried in England or the USA.

Apart from the Status of Children Act, forced on the Government by the Johnston ruling, the defeat of the referendum meant that family legislation was relegated to the bottom of the Dáil agenda.

THE 'SHATTER BILL'

In 1987 Alan Shatter introduced a Private Member's Bill, largely modelled on English divorce legislation, which would permit judges to make permanent orders regarding custody, property et cetera at one sitting. Such legislation, if enacted, would settle all matters relating to marital breakdown, but obviously could not grant the right to remarry. Prior to this some legal separations required twenty or thirty court visits, resulting in excessive monetary and psychological costs to those involved.

The Bill was opposed by the Fianna Fáil Government, who saw to it that it was watered down considerably at committee stage. It was also opposed by Family Solidarity, despite their assertions during the referendum that they would support any legislation, short of divorce, that would help those in marital breakdown situations.

In an unusual development, the Dáil referred the doctored Bill back to committee and much of the original wording was restored.

The reconstituted Bill – only the second Private Member's Bill ever to be passed in the Dáil – eventually passed by one vote to become the Judicial Separation and Family Law Reform Act, 1989.

When the results of the 1986 census were published they showed a further increase in marital breakdown (with a total figure of 37,245). What opponents of divorce had failed to address was that, despite the ban, the number of separations was rapidly increasing, as were the number of second relationships. Many of those who encountered problems looked to their local TDs for help, and it gradually became apparent that the defeat of the referendum had merely delayed dealing with the realities of marital breakdown, and that a second referendum was inevitable.

The election of Mary Robinson as President is seen by many as a watershed in Irish politics. While it would be too simplistic to say that her election was due solely to a liberal vote, none the less it was a sign of hope to many, a signal that a liberal agenda might be more realisable than it had been felt to be heretofore.

Charles J Haughey

In 1989 the then Taoiseach, Charles J Haughey TD, announced at the Fianna Fáil Ard Fheis that his government would produce a White Paper on Marital Breakdown and that this would include proposals for divorce legislation. This announcement was partially in response to the Young Turks within his own party, but was prompted mainly by the rapid increase in marital breakdown. The White Paper gestated for two years before it was grudgingly published by the Minister for Justice, Padraig Flynn. When questioned by the press, the Minister stated that he personally hoped the people would vote against divorce in a second referendum.

The White Paper itself was a hotchpotch of pro- and

anti-divorce views and, giving five different options for legislation, had more the flavour of a Green Paper. Its tone was particularly troubling in its attempts to lay blame on separating spouses and in its language of 'strict regimes'. It seems that the more conservative elements in the Department of Justice had not taken on board submissions by groups such as DAG, AIM and the Council for the Status of Women, who stated that punitive legislation would make unhappy situations worse and that attempts to lay blame were inappropriate in a mature legislation.

1991 CENSUS
The 1991 census showed a further sharp rise in separations, with the numbers of persons separated recorded as 55,143, with a further 3,856 married following the dissolution of a previous marriage. (This second figure may include annulments and foreign divorces.) While 33,793 women stated that they were separated, interestingly only 21,350 men indicated that they were. It is unclear whether the missing men have left the state or if, in second relationships, they have for tax reasons classified themselves as married. If we double the number of women, we come to a figure of 67,586, a massive increase on the 1986 census figures. This rise belies the assertion of the ADC, prior to the referendum, that rejecting divorce in Ireland would keep the floodgates closed and prevent marital breakdown.

The withdrawal of the Progressive Democrats from government precipitated an election in November of 1992. When Fianna Fáil and Labour sat down at the table to negotiate their subsequent partnership, divorce was one of the social reforms that Labour insisted on as part of the programme for government. As this programme was accepted by all TDs at the time, there was little public dissent from within government on the issue. Albert Reynolds himself seemed to be committed to backing the referendum and stated in *Business & Finance* (28 September 1994) that he believed that the Government would win the referendum in 1995.

Prior to the dramatic events of November 1994, the Minister for Equality and Law Reform, Mervyn Taylor TD, had made efforts to see enacted the raft of legislation needed in advance of a second divorce referendum. He had also indicated that the referendum was scheduled for mid 1995.

In 1986, because the government had (a) not introduced legislation to deal with the issues of division of property and finance on marital breakdown; and (b) not dealt with the status of those receiving social welfare payments after divorce, the debate on divorce became inextricably linked with these issues. The Fine Gael/Labour/Democratic Left Government's Strategy for Renewal has further reiterated that issues such as the protection of children, taxation, social welfare, inheritance and pension rights are to be fully addressed in advance of the referendum, as are improvements in the Family Mediation Service and family courts. The Government's reasoning is that if these issues have been satisfactorily clarified, then the public can focus on the fact that the only question really to be asked in a referendum is that of the right to remarry.

The years since 1986 have seen a gradual shift in public opinion. Tragic cases have impressed on the public that the family can be a dangerous place for some. The influence of the church has also waned, and events such as Bishop Eamon Casey's fall from grace have given pause for thought to many. It is particularly ironic that Bishop Casey, who was popular and charismatic, and who undoubtedly had a major influence on the public, was one of the foremost opponents of divorce in 1986. This, we now know, was while he was concealing the fact that he had had an affair with a divorcee, and that he had fathered a child. Yet the Bishop preached against those who wished to divorce, some precisely because they wanted legally to marry the father/mother of their child.

The debate around the Maastricht Protocol and subsequent referenda also highlighted the narrow thinking of Family Solidarity (aka ADC) and illustrated the truism that the mere fact of a vote against the introduction of divorce, or any other social issue, does not exorcise the problems that caused the pressure for a vote in the first place.

Hopefully the recent shifts in public opinion will stand the test of a second referendum on divorce. Those of us who were involved in the first campaign can now look on it as a dry run for the next, we know the issues, we know the pitfalls and we know it can be won.

The outcome will depend largely on the willingness of the present Government and all parties in the Dáil to give their

Mags O'Brien

whole-hearted commitment to the forthcoming campaign. If the genuine fears and confusion that people had in 1986 and which, to a large extent, they still have, are taken seriously, it is vital that the public at large are informed of the real issues that surround marital breakdown and of the changes in the law and in social welfare codes since 1986. People must now realise that a vote against divorce will not stop marital breakdown; rather it will only exacerbate the problems that are faced by those separating or in second relationships.

Marital breakdown is a sad and very real fact of life in Ireland today. How we assist those whose marriages are in difficulty or irretrievably broken down reflects the type of society we really are. Do we care for all our families or just the constitutional ones?

REFERENCES

Brady, John SJ, *Studies*, Autumn 1986.

Chubb, Basil, *Government and Politics of Ireland*, Dublin: Gill & McMillan, 1991.

Divorce Action Group, *A Case For Divorce*, Dublin: 1986.

Faludi, Susan, *Backlash: The Undeclared War Against Women*, London: Chatto & Windus, 1992.

Fine-Davis, Margaret, *Changing Gender Role Attitudes in Ireland: 1975-1986*, Volume III. Attitudes towards Moral Issues in Relation to Voting Behaviour in Recent Referenda. 2nd Commission Report 1988.

FitzGerald, Garret, *All In A Life: An Autobiography*, Dublin: Gill & McMillan, 1991.

Glenn, Alice, *The Alice Glenn Report*, Vol 1 No.3. 1986.

Grimes, Richard, and Horgan: *Introduction to Law in the Republic of Ireland*, Dublin: Wolfhound Press, 1981.

MacCurtain, Margaret and Donncha O'Corrain, *Women in Irish Society: The Historical Dimension*, Dublin: Arlen House, 1978.

O'Reilly, Emily, *Masterminds of the Right*, Dublin: Attic Press, 1992.

Stationery Office, *Report of the Committee on the Constitution*, Dublin: 1967.

Stationery Office, *Joint Oireachtas Committee on Marital Breakdown*, Dublin: 1985.

Tuohy, Frank, *Yeats: An Illustrated Biography*. London: Herbert Press, 1976.

Walsh, Dick, 'If anyone could get it, everyone would want it', *Irish Times* 7 February 1986.

Weitzman, Leonore J, *The Divorce Revolution*, New York: The Free Press, 1985.

Reasons for Marital Instability and Separation

Finóla Ó Riagáin

INTRODUCTION

The traditional institution of marriage is changing rapidly in practically every Western state (Hall 1993, Furstenberg 1990). Two aspects of the change have become topics of almost constant public debate. There is evidence of a growing degree of dissatisfaction within marriage; of instability, breakdown, separation and (where permitted) divorce and remarriage. Secondly, among the unmarried adult population there appears to be an increase in the proportion of people who have decided to cohabit rather than marry, and/or to bear and raise children outside marriage.

The reasons for these changes, and the possible connections between them, are by no means clear. Among the factors that cloud and confuse the issue are differences between states and cultures. Rates of marital instability would appear to be much higher in, for example, the United States of America than in western Europe, despite broad similarities in state laws governing the dissolution of marriage. In similar vein, the rise in rates of cohabitation is held to be a consequence of divorce in Britain, but it is also increasing in Ireland, where divorce is prohibited. Thus, while national differences in the legal provisions governing the dissolution of marriage may be a factor in explaining international variations in marital instability, other economic, social and cultural (including religious) differences may, in combination, be more important.

However, there appears to be general agreement that two large-scale social shifts, which are probably related to each other, have deeply influenced marriage trends and patterns. The first of these is the growing trend to which women, especially married women, are entering or remaining in the workforce. This has reduced the degree to which women are economically dependent on marriage. The second factor is the growing belief that marriage should be based on companionship and love rather than on the need to ensure reproductive survival (Hopflinger 1991, see also Dominion 1984 and Gittins 1993). The shift in perspective from marriage as an institution to marriage as a relationship has had profound implications. The standard has moved from one in which couples were expected to remain in marriages even if they were not in love with one another to one which increasingly accepts the legitimacy of separation unless the couples are 'in love'.

Within these macro-social changes, research had identified other factors which contribute to the stability or instability of marriage. These include: age at marriage; the duration of marriage; the presence of children, especially young children; the incidence of marital instabiliy among parents of married couples; social class; the marriage laws in the particular jurisdiction; and a range of other religious, cultural and psychological factors (see Burgoyne *et al.* 1987, Morgan and Rindfuss 1985 and Furstenberg 1990 for a review of the literature.) However, whether and to what extent any one of these factors will be present in a specific country and how it will interact with others is a matter to be determined by empirical investigation. National experiences are not a simple reflection of global processes. Therefore, in considering the reasons for marital instability and separation in Ireland, both the extent to which the Irish experience reflects and deviates from the international pattern must be considered.

DATA ON MARITAL BREAKDOWN IN IRELAND

There are several statistical measures of the scale of marital breakdown in Ireland. They do not reflect the full picture, as measures of the dissolution of a relationship (separation in Ireland/divorce elsewhere) do not, and cannot of their nature measure the degree to which marriages have become 'unstable'. Booth *et al.* (1984) define marital instability as marriages in which disharmony has reached the point that at least one partner is seriously considering separation and has taken preliminary actions to that end by talking to a counsellor, legal adviser et cetera. They point out that while marital instability, so defined, may lead to separation, this is not necessarily the case, and its full incidence is thus not reflected by separation statistics alone.

Nevertheless, official statistics of separation do provide a starting point. According to the Census of Population in 1991 (Vol.II) the number of married persons in Ireland increased by two per cent in the five years since 1986. During the same period, however, the number of separated persons increased by 48 per cent to 55,143 persons. Of those reported as separated in 1991, 43 per cent were deserted, 24 per cent were living informally apart, 11 per cent were divorced, two per cent had annulments and 20 per cent had legal separations. In total, only one third of those living apart from their spouses had either a legal separation, divorce or annulment. This is not surprising given the high cost of legal proceedings and the absence of an adequate legal-aid system in this country. Despite this, and even though the numbers are small, the applications for judicial separations have increased dramatically since the Judicial Separation and Family Law Reform Act (1989) was introduced. In 1988/89 there were 207 applications for judicial separation; the following year the figure had trebled to 623 (Marital Breakdown 1992, Appendix 3.3). Together with the increase in applications for judicial separations, the social-welfare payments to deserted wives (since 1991 known as the Lone Parent's Allowance) has increased by 66 per cent during the five-year period 1986-1991 (Marital Breakdown 1992, Appendix 3.11).

In the same period the marriage rate per 1,000 of the population has dropped from 5.2 to 4.8, while the proportion of births outside marriage has risen steadily and now accounts for 18 per cent of all births and nearly one in three of first-time births. In the absence of a direct measure of cohabitation, the combination of these two statistics suggests that it too is increasing rapidly in Ireland.

However, the little official data available to date can do no more than broadly indicate the scale of the problem and the direction and rate of change. Very little can be inferred from the data as to the reasons for marital instability in Ireland. For this purpose, the most useful sources of data are those collected by the agencies to whom couples with marital difficulties turn to for advice, couselling and mediation assistance. Unfortunately, not much of this data has been analysed or published, and this paper concentrates on the one source available to me, the data collected by the AIM group at its Dublin centre over the years 1988 to 1993. Since 1972, the AIM group has provided non-directive counselling, legal information, a referral and, more recently, a mediation service to people with marriage and family problems.

Information obtained from clients who call to the centre includes data on marital status, age, occupation, kinds of marital problems encountered, home ownership and professional help sought by clients. While this data lacks the comprehensive coverage provided by official sources or large-scale surveys, it is, none the less, one of the most informative of currently available sources about the social factors associated with marital instability and its causes as perceived by those involved. With nearly 2,000 cases, the data set is relatively large, and comparison with census figures for the Dublin area suggests that there is no undue bias in favour of any particular age or social group. More importantly, the data form a coherent picture of marital instability and breakdown that compares well with the research findings in other countries. The Irish situation is not, of course, identical, but the differences are readily explained by differences in the Irish legal, social and cultural context. In the remainder of this chapter I will briefly outline these patterns and compare them with international research findings.

TRENDS

While the AIM centre is open for only three hours each morning, and only in Dublin, there has been a dramatic increase in the number of clients contacting the centre over the last five years. There was an increase of 41 per cent in the number of callers to the centre since 1989 (Table 1).

Table 1: PERSONAL AND TELEPHONE CONSULTATIONS AT AIM CENTRE (DUBLIN) 1989–1993

Year	Personal	Telephone
Jan 89–Oct 89 (8 months)	196	718
Nov 89–Oct 90	379	1531
Nov 90–Oct 91	300	1113
Nov 91–Oct 92	474	1579
Nov 92–Oct 93	533	1778
Total	**1882**	**6719**

(*Source*: Annual Statistical Reports: AIM Centre)

While allowing for the limitations of these figures, the direction and rate of change is consistent with the other sources referred to above. The majority of AIM clients are women. Although this may reflect a public perception of AIM as a women's organisation, the proportion of male clients, currently around 20 per cent, is slowly increasing. The predominance of women, therefore, is more likely to reflect the well-established international pattern for women to be the primary instigators of separation proceedings (Dominion 1984). This is the case despite the fact that women are frequently, if not mostly, the more vulnerable partner in the event of a separation.

SOCIO-DEMOGRAPHIC CHARACTERISTICS

Age

The age profile of AIM clients reflects the general age structure of the Dublin adult married population, ie about half are under 40 years. But a more detailed breakdown shows some deviations which are hardly surprising. People considering some action in relation to their marital problems tend to be in their middle years, rather than very young or very old. Nearly 40 per cent of clients are in their forties, compared to 23 per cent in the general population. Furthermore, although only four per cent of clients are over 60 (compared to 24 per cent of all married persons in this age group), their presence indicates that marital breakdown occurs in even the longest established marriages.

Employment status

'In legal terms, inequalities are often written into the marital relationship defining the status of the wife as dependant' (Land 1975), but this is slowly changing, even 'if the expectation remains that the male job is primary'. Just over one third of wives (either clients or wives of clients) work full-time in the home, but only about one half of those in the labour force are in full-time employment. Furthermore, of wives who work full-time, just under 30 per cent are in occupations which the Central Statistics Office ranks among the top socio-economic groups (ie professional, managerial and salaried employees). By comparison, more than three quarters of husbands are in full-time occupations and are more likely (40 per cent) to be found in the top socio-economic groups as defined above. An average of 15 per cent of clients, over the last three years, have said that the husband was unemployed at the time. This compares closely with the national rate.

Socio-economic group

Because relatively large numbers of wives are either not in the labour force or in part-time occupations, social class was based on the husband's occupation. With the exception of the semi- and unskilled occupational categories, AIM clients are drawn from all socio-economic groups. It is not possible directly to compare this occupation-based class distribution with census figures as the figures for the Dublin area do not distinguish between married and single persons. However, in very general terms, it would appear that the socio-economic distribution of AIM clients is broadly comparable for the top socio-economic catergories, somewhat over-represented in the middle categories and under-represented in the lower. The under-representation of this last group may reflect the relatively lower marriage rates among males in these social categories, as well as a lower propensity to resort to the legal system for the resolution of marriage difficulties. Pending further research on this issue it can be tentatively concluded that marital instability is a feature of marriages in all socio-economic groups.

Marital status

Nearly all AIM clients were married or had been married, but only slightly over half were formally or informally separated. However, only 21 per cent of those living apart from their spouses had a legal separation, a divorce or a state annulment. Furthermore, the fact that nearly half of AIM clients were still living in the marital relationship suggests that the census figures – which report only people who have actually separated – considerably underestimate the full extent of marital instability.

Children

Over 90 per cent of clients have at least one child and about half have three or more children. While researchers seem divided as to whether children act as a stress or a bonding factor in a marriage (Waite and Lillard 1991), it is clear that the timing of the decision to separate is directly related to the presence of children. Research conducted by Burgoyne *et al.* (1987) indicates that the median duration for childless divorcing couples was eight years compared to eleven years for couples who had at least one child, and they conclude that although children do not necessarily cement a marriage, their presence seems to delay its legal end. The evidence strongly suggests that this is the case with AIM clients in Dublin.

Number of years married
As shown in Table 2, fewer than one quarter of clients are less than ten years married, and over 40 per cent are married for more than 20 years.

Years married	%
1–5 years	8
5–10 years	15
10–15 years	20
15–20 years	15
20–30 years	34
Over 30 years	8
Total	**100**

(*Source*: Annual Statistics Report: AIM Centre)

The duration of marriage, when considered with the data on children, prompts the conclusion that separation is very much a last resort for most of the AIM clients.

REASONS FOR MARITAL BREAKDOWN

Nature of marital problems
Although AIM primarily offers advice and counselling on the legal aspects of marital breakdown, it is generally necessary to establish the basic problem within the relationship as that, of course, has legal as well as interpersonal implications. When asked, clients usually cited several factors (Table 3).

TABLE 3: NATURE OF MARITAL PROBLEMS CITED BY CLIENT

Nature of Problem	%
Communication	47
Personality	40
Incompatibility	35
Alcohol	30
Financial	28
Infidelity	25
Sexual	23
Violence	21
Other	10

Note: figures do not add to 100% because many clients cite more than one problem.

(*Source:* Annual Statistics Reports: AIM Centre)

Because of the obviously subjective nature of these assessments – which are always made by the client – it is the overall pattern rather than the specific frequency of any one item which is of most interest. The most frequently mentioned problems – communication, personality disorders and incompatibility – all point to a general breakdown in the marriage relationship. In the case of a significant minority, the problems take a more specific form and the frequently associated problems of violence and alcoholism are mentioned by about one quarter of clients. Infidelity is also mentioned by one quarter of clients. A similar proportion mention financial problems as being among the causes of marital breakdown, and while this may be due to low incomes or unemployment, there appear to be many cases in which the pattern of money management within marriage gives rise to serious inequalities and even hardship, especially for women (Oakley 1989). But the main point concerning the marital problems listed in Table 3 is that they are often present in some combination rather than singly.

Statistics reported by the Cork branch of the Catholic

Marriage and Advisory Service are in broad accord with the figures cited above (*Irish Times* 1993). The report notes that in 1992, among the 2,226 couples who consulted the centre, 29 per cent suspected infidelity by one of the partners, 56 per cent reported alcohol abuse and 44 per cent physical violence. Overall, in the case of 'at least' 50 per cent of the couples approaching the centre during the year, the centre found that 'chronically dysfunctional communication skills had already led to severe marital conflict'. Similarly, the most common problems dealt with by the Marriage Counselling Service (MCS 1992) in Dublin were communication (61 per cent) and personality traits (51 per cent). Among other problems with which comparisons can be made were infidelity (20 per cent), financial (19 per cent), alcohol/violence (18 per cent). Bearing in mind that these two bodies are marriage-counselling agencies and that AIM typically sees people who have moved to the point of considering legal rather than counselling solutions to their problems, there would appear to be a consid-erable degree of consistency between the three sources in terms of the marital problems they identified.

Research in other countries is usually based on the reasons cited in divorce proceedings, and this makes com-parisons difficult. As Burgoyne *et al.* (1978) have pointed out, this data should be interpreted with great caution because couples or individuals petitioning for divorce tend to present their 'reason' in terms that will advance their case. Nevertheless, these authors note that the rise in petitions using the behaviour of the partner as grounds for divorce is also reflected in survey evidence. In particular, they note survey findings indicating that 20–40 per cent of divorced women claim that physical violence was among the causes of the breakdown of the marriage.

WHEN DO MARITAL PROBLEMS BEGIN?
The high average duration of the marriage not withstanding (Table 2 above), 40 per cent of clients say that their marital problems began within the first year of their marriage or at the very beginning, and as many as 60 per cent place the initial problems in the first five years.

TABLE 4: WHEN DID MARITAL PROBLEMS BEGIN?

Year of Marriage	%
First year	39
1–5 years	19
5–10 years	14
10–20 years	21
20 plus years	7
Total	100

(*Source*: Annual Statistics Reports: AIM Centre)

Again, this finding accords very closely with the international research evidence (Morgan and Rindfuss 1985). According to Dominion (1984), during the first five years of a marriage, between 30 and 40 per cent of all marital breakdown occurs and basic difficulties in the relationship become apparent, although actual breakdown may not occur for up to 20 years.

PROFESSIONAL HELP SOUGHT BY CLIENTS
Not only have a large proportion of AIM clients coped with their marital difficulties for a very long time, but most have resorted to outside assistance. A large majority (87 per cent) of clients have sought professional help before coming to AIM, and some have been to several agencies (Table 5).

TABLE 5: PROFESSIONAL HELP SOUGHT BY AIM CLIENTS

Category of Help	%
Counselling	49
Legal	30
Medical	23
AA	13
None	13
Religious	10
Other	6

Note: figures do not add to 100% because many clients cite more than one form of assistance.

(*Source*: Annual Statistics Reports: AIM Centre)

Nearly half of all clients had already tried marriage counselling. Viewed in the context of other findings, these figures suggest a very high commitment to marriage among the clients, and a determination to try many possible solutions before resorting to legal processes. None the less, while clients sought and received information on many aspects of family law in their consultation with AIM, nearly two thirds sought information on marital separation. It would appear that none of these supporting agencies, either individually or in combination, were able to help the couples resolve their marital problems.

CONCLUSIONS

A short chapter cannot, of course, review all aspects of the causes and trends in marital breakdown, and the present state of Irish research in the area permits only tentative conclusions. However, it would appear that the causes of marital breakdown in Ireland reflect the growing worldwide concern with the quality of the marital relationship itself. While there is evidence that external factors such as extra-marital affairs and financial difficulties were important, the dominant problems were in the areas of communication and personality disorders. In the case of a sizeable minority, these problems were to be found in combination with alcohol and/or violence.

The most significant difference between the Irish experience and that of other countries concerns the duration of marriage. While the evidence strongly suggests that marital problems emerge at a very early stage in a marriage, most Irish couples struggle with the difficulty for many years. This may be due to the higher birth rate in Ireland, the more economically dependent position of women within marriage and the difficulty, until recently, of finding a satisfactory legal solution. All of these factors are now changing. Thus, although the base is currently small, a continuation of the present intercensal rate of increase would suggest a projected figure of over 100,000 separated persons by 2001. But legislative and other changes could accelerate the rate of increase. The AIM data alone indicate that census data seriously underestimate the true extent of marital breakdown in Ireland, perhaps by a factor of two or more.

Nor can the reason for marital breakdown be disassociated with the related questions as to why declining numbers of people are either not marrying or postponing marriage, or why the rate of cohabitation and births outside marriage is increasing. Taken together, all these factors signal a substantial shift in traditional values and patterns. It is no longer possible to assume the stability of the conjugal unit or even that child-bearing will be regulated by marriage. Not much thought or public attention has been given to whether it is possible to strengthen the institution of marriage and/or parental arrangements that are the functional equivalent of marriage. While governments cannot restore traditional family structures, they can influence the wellbeing of children and families by policies that are responsive to family life. Such policies might include better child care, parental leave, more flexible employment practices and, of course, reducing unemployment (Cherlin 1988). In addition, Dominion *et al.* would stress the need for more and better education in personal relationships.

However, the data presented in this chapter would suggest that such policies will, at best, be a very long-term solution and may never be more than partially effective. Nor does the evidence reviewed here suggest that marriage counselling will greatly ameliorate the trends. Although research now becoming available in other countries indicates that it is difficult to define provisions for dealing with the consequences of divorce, 'it is even more difficult to invent ways of rejuvenating commitment to marriage or promoting the stability of existing family units' (Furstenberg 1990).

REFERENCES

Booth, A *et al.*, 'Women Outside Employment and Marital Instability'. *American Journal of Sociology*, 90, 567-83, 1984.

Burgoyne, J *et al.*, *Divorce Matters*, Harmondsworth: Penguin, 1987.

Census of Population 1991, Vol. II Ages and Marital Status, Dublin: Government Publications Office, 1987.

Cherlin, A (ed.), *The Changing Face of American Public Policy*, Washington: Urban Institute Press, 1988.

Dominion, J, 'Marital Breakdown and the Future of the Family'. *Long-Range Planning*, 17,2, 77-84, 1984.

Dominion, J *et al.*, *Marital Breakdown and the Health of the Nation*, London: One plus One, Marriage and Partnership Research, 1991.

Furstenberg, F F, 'Divorce and the American Family', *Annual Review of Sociology*. Vol. 16, 379-403.

Gittins, D, *The Family in Question*. London: MacMillan, 1993.

Hall, R, 'Family Structures'. In Noin, D. and Woods, R., *The Changing Population of Europe*, 100-126, Oxford: Blackwell, 1993.

Hopflinger, F, 'The Future of Household and Family Structures in Europe', Proceedings of a Seminar on Present Demographic Trends and Lifestyles in Europe, Sept 1991. Strasbourg: Council of Europe, 1991.

Irish Times, 3 March 1993.

Land, F, 'The Myth of the Male Breadwinner', *New Society*, Oct 71-3, 1975.

Marital Breakdown: A review and proposed changes (White Paper). Dublin: Government Publications, 1992.

(MCS) Marriage Counselling Services Annual Report 1992, Dublin.

Morgan, S and Rindfuss, R, 'Marital Disruption: Structural and Temporal Dimensions', *American Journal of Sociology*, 90,5, 1055-77 1985.

Oakley, A, 'Women's Studies in British Sociology', *British Journal of Sociology*, 40,3, 442-470, 1989.

Waite, L J and Lilliard, L A, 'Children and Marital Disruption'. *American Journal of Sociology*. 96,4, 930-953, 1991.

Marital Breakdown and Divorce

The psychological consequences for adults and their children

Dr Sheila Greene

In this chapter I will identify some of the central issues to be considered before conclusions can be drawn about the effects of marital breakdown and divorce on adults and their children. I will then summarise some of the research findings on this topic, bearing in mind their inevitable limitations.

CULTURAL AND HISTORICAL CONTEXT

It is not possible to generalise with any validity about marriage, or about problems with marriage and the solution to those problems. The customs and ideologies surrounding marriage are specific to both culture and historical period. From this point of view there is an immediate difficulty in using research carried out in other countries and at other times to help us predict the human consequences of divorce, if it were to be introduced in Ireland in the mid-1990s.

Marital breakdown is already a reality for many Irish families. In the 1991 census, 55,143 people described themselves as separated (Ward, 1993). It is clear that at the moment, the Irish rate of marital breakdown is not as high as those obtaining in other Western societies such as the UK, where one in three marriages ends in divorce, and the USA, where one in two marriages ends in divorce (Wallerstein and Blakeslee, 1989), but it does appear to be rising. We do not know the number of Irish marriages which are a source of distress to the men and women involved in them, but we have no reason to assume that levels of marital discord are any different from those found in other Western countries.

Irish resistance to divorce is not an historical accident, but is a consequence of deeply held convictions on the part of the majority of its citizens about the religious basis of moral authority, the nature of the family and its responsibilities to children. As will be clear from other chapters of this book, such attitudes and beliefs are no doubt shaped by the economic and social realities of Irish culture. Irish society is changing, and the attitudes of Irish citizens towards marriage are also changing (Fine-Davis, 1988). The introduction of divorce would be a clear index of the extent of that change but, if it is introduced, it will be divorce Irish-style. Ireland will still be a small, religiously and racially homogeneous country, with its own distinctive strengths and weaknesses. This country may never experience levels of divorce comparable to those reached in our neighbouring island: it is impossible to predict.

Ireland may prove capable of protecting its citizens against the negative economic, social and psychological consequences of divorce while emphasising the positive consequences. That, too, is impossible to predict, but we do not have much reason to be sanguine when we look at our response to marital breakdown to date. The social changes which have taken place in Ireland over the last few decades require a transformation in official attitudes and policies in relation to the family. An examination of studies of the psychological effects of divorce and marital breakdown on adults and children in other cultures conveys the strong message that these psychological consequences are mediated by culturally specific attitudes to marital breakdown, lone parents, lone adults, working mothers, the role of mothers and of fathers and, very importantly, how much responsibility the community or the state is prepared to take in ensuring that the adults and children involved in a broken marriage are not inevitably going to suffer. Bilge and Kaufman (1983) describe cultures, such as those of Hopi native Americans and the Hadza tribe in Africa, where most marriages end in divorce but where, because of the highly communal way of life and the lack of stigma attached to divorce, the lives of adults and children change very little as a result and they appeared to suffer little distress or disadvantage.

In Ireland we do not appear to have changed our attitudes and policies in a way that might accommodate the new family structures and patterns that are emerging in Irish society (McCullagh, 1991). We are, therefore, at the moment not well-equipped to support families which break down or families which are structured in non-traditional ways. We cannot cling to a vision of the Irish family as consisting of working father, mother at home and 4.5 children in this time of high unemployment and increasing numbers of working mothers, never-married parents, broken marriages, lone parents, and a rapidly declining birth-rate. Part of the social change is the increasing unwillingness of men and women to stay in unhappy marriages.

These changes are in themselves neither good nor bad, but their consequences will not be positive unless politicians and policy-makers show flexibility, adaptability and a willingness to face the realities of the plural nature of Irish families in the 1990s, and the nature of their needs.

INDIVIDUAL DIFFERENCES

Just as it is unjustified to generalise about the effects of marital breakdown and divorce across cultures, it is dangerous to generalise about the effects of marital breakdown and divorce for individuals within a culture.

It is obvious that the experience of adults and children caught up in the marital break-up process will be different, but all adults and all children will certainly not react alike. The nature of the process itself will vary in its duration and predictability, and in the amount of conflict and disruption inflicted on all concerned. How these factors operate is in turn dependent on the life history and personality of the individuals involved, and on their coping capacities, social supports and wider social circumstances.

Although attitudes to marital breakdown are, as discussed above, likely to reflect the dominant ideologies of the culture, at an individual level there is still considerable scope for difference. Thus one woman may construe the breakdown of her marriage as evidence of a deep personal failure while another may see it as evidence of her newfound strength and independence. Children, too, will vary in their capacity to cope with the changes they confront, whether it be because of temperamental or acquired vulnerability or resilience.

Research into the effects of marital breakdown has shown the importance of consideration of the individual's developmental context. The meaning of events and therefore their probable psychological impact varies according to the person's age. This is very evident in childhood where developmental changes are dramatic, but is also true in adulthood when, for example, the meaning of divorce will be entirely different to a man of 57 than it is to a man of 27.

A number of studies has shown gender to be another critically important variable. Not only do men and women tend to react differently to marital breakdown – a finding that is entirely predictable given the differing functions marriage serves for men and women – but girls and boys also tend to react in different ways. Other differences, such as those of class and membership of a subculture, like that of the travellers, are also likely to be important.

MARITAL DISCORD VERSUS MARITAL BREAKDOWN AND DIVORCE

When attempting to pinpoint the psychological effects of marital breakdown or divorce, it is very difficult to establish whether or not the observed effects are due to the experiences associated with chronic discord or to those specific to breakdown, since breakdown or divorce very rarely occur without a substantial period of discord. Some light can be cast on this issue by looking at what is known about the effects of living with marital discord.

Studies investigating the origins of a whole range of psychological disorders in adults and children have found a strong negative effect of marital discord (Quinton and Rutter, 1985; Burgoyne, Ormrod and Richards, 1987). Some of the reported negative psychological effects of separation and divorce are undoubtedly the effects of pre-divorce conflict or of continuing post-divorce conflict between parents.

Since divorce is now so common in the USA and the UK it is increasingly possible to use data from longitudinal studies of originally intact families. For example, Block, Block and Gjerde (1986) report evidence from the California Growth Study of behavioural problems and lack of parental control evident in boys for as long as eleven years before the parents divorced, and not found at the same level in families which remained intact. Elliot and Richards (1991) examined data from the National Child Development Survey in the UK, which involved the follow-up of 17,000 children born in 1958, and concluded that 'some of the problems which have been attributed to divorce/separation in previous cross-sectional studies may in fact be present prior to parental separation'.

A related issue is the extent to which children might be less damaged by living in a home where there is marital conflict than by suffering the consequences of parental separation and divorce. According to Rutter and Rutter (1992), psychological disturbance is as common in families where there are significant levels of marital discord as it is in families which have broken up. An empirical study carried out by Emery (1982) found that children function better in conflict-free divorced families than in conflict-ridden two-parent families. In interpreting these findings, however, it must be borne in mind that many divorces are not conflict-free.

Amato and Keith (1991) reviewed nine studies which permitted a comparison between children in high-conflict families and children whose parents had divorced, and concluded that high levels of conflict had a more pernicious effect on children's psychological adjustment than family status *per se*. Amato and Keith comment: 'Children in divorced families appear to have a higher level of wellbeing than do children in high-conflict intact families' (p.40).

The findings of the Exeter Family Study in the UK received a lot of media attention in 1994 (Joseph Rowntree Foundation, 1994). The authors of this preliminary, brief report claim that 'Although severe marital conflict and financial hardship were associated with poor outcomes for children, family re-organisation seemed to be the main adverse factor in children's lives'. In the study, 152 children and their parents were inter-viewed. Half of the children were living with both biological parents, and half had experienced their parents' divorce or sepa-ration. Children in families re-ordered by divorce or separation reported more problems, and these reports were confirmed in the interviews with their parents. The number of problems increased according to the number of family transitions which had occured after the initial divorce or separation. Of the children living in intact families, those experiencing high levels of marital conflict between their parents did not exibit levels of distress or maladjustment found in the children whose parents had divorced, although they did have more problems than the children in intact families where there was no evident marital conflict. It was this finding that was most widely cited as evidence for the view that children were better off when parents stay together in conflict than when parents divorce.

This conclusion contradicts that reached by other researchers, such as those mentioned above. It is not yet possible to evaluate the scientific standing of the Exeter study, since the details of the study have not been published.

Despite the fact that many studies show that marital discord in intact families is associated with high levels of problems for both adults and children, a number of researchers have reported that most children of a broken marriage would prefer their parents to stay together no matter what (Wallerstein and Kelly, 1980). This occurs despite the evidence that children, even in infancy, are very sensitive to their parents' rows and very upset by them (Cummings, Iannotti and Zahn-Waxler, 1985). Children clearly find it very difficult to tolerate the dismantling of their family, no matter how destructive and disturbing that family life might be for them. A conclusion that might be drawn from these apparently conflicting findings is that when parents cease to be a couple, it is important to find a way for the child to continue to hold on to his or her family. It seems that the child's attachment to both parents and to the sense of their own family rarely dies, and that their understandable grief at the breakdown at their parents' marriage is coloured by their fears about the destruction of their family, as she or he experiences it.

MARITAL BREAKDOWN VERSUS DIVORCE

There is very little evidence on the comparative effects of marital breakdown, legal separation and divorce. In countries which permit divorce, most people with broken marriages avail of it.

A greater frequency of re-marriages is one inevitable consequence of divorce, and one which distinguishes it from legal separation. Re-marriage brings its own parcel of positive and negative changes. Studies carried out in the USA indicate that adults who re-marry experience a great improvement in wellbeing for some time – despite the fact that the eventual divorce rate for second marriages (60 per cent in the USA, 50 per cent in the UK) is higher than that for first marriages (Burgoyne, Ormrod and Richards, 1987). Pre-adolescent boys often appear to do better with a male step-parent than they did living with their mother alone, but girls, particularly those who are emotionally close to their mothers, can react badly to the intrusion of a step-father (Hetherington, 1989; Clingempeel and Segal, 1986). The fact that the least positive outcomes for second marriages occur where both partners have offspring from previous marriages is an example of how deeply entangled are the lives of parents and children.

Many of the psychological consequences of marital breakdown and divorce are shared. It is hard to see in what way divorce could worsen the lives of those involved in an irretrievably broken-down marriage: it might make the situation easier by the introduction of greater clarity and the freedom for the adults to form a new family without stigma. If the Irish government, upon the introduction of divorce, were to set out to take the fact of marital breakdown and its consequences seriously in terms of the provision of services and resources and appropriate legislative support, the families involved might have a real possibility of faring better than they would have done in the absence of divorce.

Those who are opposed to divorce might argue that it will add to the sum total of human misery by encouraging people to separate who might not otherwise have done so. The spectre of casual and irresponsible divorce is a real one, and it undoubtedly does occur, but most of the evidence available from other countries suggests that the majority of couples struggle to keep their marriages alive, particularly when children are involved (Emery, 1988). Unfortunately, the irresponsible desertion of spouse and children is also a phenomenon which is well established in Ireland, divorce or no divorce. In 1991 11,358 women were in receipt of the Deserted Wife's Benefit (Ward, 1993).

DIRECT AND INDIRECT CONSEQUENCES OF MARITAL BREAKDOWN AND DIVORCE

Some of the troubling consequences of marital breakdown and divorce are not directly caused by those events. They are coincidental with or consequential upon marital breakdown and divorce, but arise mainly because of the way a particular society responds to divorce. The essential characteristics of the situation are that when a marriage breaks up, the married couple separates and the child no longer has her or his two parents living together in the one house. Adults, even those who welcome the separation, will mourn the death of that marriage, and may find it difficult to break their psychological attachment to their erstwhile partner, even if the relationship has become characterised more by hatred than love (Weiss, 1975). For the adults, more than this has been lost in a society like ours where a successful, heterosexual marriage is upheld as on one of life's major goals. We have also come to invest in marriage much of our expectations for companionship, and social life is still generally structured around the concept of enduring marriage.

The children will often grieve for the loss of the security of having two parents available to them. They, too, in our society expect a family to contain a mother and a father living together. They will worry about their parents and about themselves and feel the brunt of their parents' psychological turmoil and preoccupation. Some of the worst of these psychological effects can be mitigated by the best efforts of the adults in the family, and by the support of the extended family and friends, but some level of distress and sadness seems inevitable, alongside the more positive reactions like relief (Wallerstein and Kelly, 1980).

What is not necessary is that families should feel stigmatised, that lone fathers or mothers should experience financial hardship, and that they should be offered very little support in fulfilling their functions as parents. When the effects of marital breakdown and divorce are reviewed it is often very difficult to disentangle the direct from the indirect effects. It is clear, however, that much of the distress and hardship is not inevitable.

MYTHS AND METHODS

Given the extent of the problem of marital breakdown in this country, there is surprisingly little research into the topic. Although there are some Irish studies which refer to the effects of family adversity on children (eg Jeffers and Fitzgerald, 1991; Sheehan and Byrne, 1989), or which discuss the changing nature of marriage and the family in Ireland (eg Hannan, 1973; Clancy, 1985), there is very little work on the factors which sustain or destroy Irish marriages and on the actual experiences of Irish parents and children. In this situation we are obliged to turn to studies carried out in other countries and sometimes fail to bear in mind, as noted above, their cultural and historical specificity.

What is also often forgotten in relation to these studies is that many of them have major methodological limitations. Cross-sectional studies can be informative, but they do not address the fact that divorce is 'best conceptualised as a process of change which extends over time' (Emery, 1988), and will fail to capture the natural history of individual responses to this process.

Longitudinal studies are therefore of particular value, but a number of the most often cited studies, for example the Virginia Longitudinal Study of Divorce and Remarriage (Hetherington, Cox and Cox, 1982; Hetherington, 1989) and the California Children of Divorce Study (Wallerstein and Kelly, 1980; Wallerstein and Blakeslee, 1989) involved small, unrepresentative samples. This is not to say that the insights gained from these studies should be ignored – this is far from the case since it was studies such as these which highlighted the complexity of the divorce process and the variability of responses to it – but it does suggest that caution should be exercised in generalising from their specific findings.

Where good empirical studies are missing, it is tempting to rely on the views of those professionals who work closely with adults and children involved in broken marriages. Although the opinions and insights of psychotherapists, psychiatrists, clinical and counselling psychologists, marriage counsellors et cetera are of inestimable value, the intrinsic bias in their perspective must be kept in mind. They are likely to overemphasise the negative consequences of marital breakdown, because, by definition, they see only those adults and children who are in trouble.

In the absence of evidence on the Irish situation there is also a tendency to rely on myth, even myth couched in terms such as 'studies have shown that...'. For example, the view is often expressed that the distress experienced by children when parents divorce is due to the fact that children inevitably blame themselves for the breakdown of the relationship. There is no evidence of self-blame being central to the response of children beyond pre-school age, nor is self-blame found in all young children. Burgoyne, Ormrod and Richards (1987) suggest that 'the widespread belief that children bear such feelings of responsibility despite evidence to the contrary is perhaps an indication of what parents would prefer to believe about the origins of their child's unhappiness'. Another myth is the view that children need their mothers more than they need their fathers – what Emery (1988) has called the 'tender years presumption' has been widely maintained and has had major implications for child-custody arrangements, despite the evidence that children need contact with both parents and that where physical custody has to be primarily with one parent, boys, in particular, are often better adjusted when in the custody of their fathers (Warshak and Santrock, 1983).

I will attempt a necessarily very brief summary of some of the more consistent and reliable findings from the literature on the psychological effects of marital separation and divorce, bearing in mind the problems I have delineated in generalising about a topic as complex and heterogeneous as marital breakdown, and bearing in mind that there is a large gap between what we understand and what we need to understand. Since most of the literature cited is on divorce, I will not refer to other forms of marital breakdown, but the processes involved are common for the most part.

ADULTS: SHORT-TERM EFFECTS

Each partner of a marriage sees that marriage very differently at the best of times, and although in many troubled marriages the fact that there are marital problems is out in the open, there may well be failure to agree about the nature of these problems and the possible solutions to them. Equally, some people are unaware of the extent of their partner's dissatisfaction until the moment she or he announces they want the marriage to end.

The manner in which the decision to divorce is arrived at – whether it is welcome or unwelcome, sudden or long-anticipated, accompanied by anger and violence or by coldness and silence – will colour the entire divorce process and its outcome for each of the partners to the marriage (Kelly, 1982).

Despite these differences, most adults experience divorce as a major life stressor. The peak time of their distress may vary according to their role in the divorce process: not surprisingly the spouse who is taken by surprise at the unwelcome announcement of the other spouse's wish for a divorce will experience most shock, anger and depression after that time, whereas their partner may have been most stressed before arriving at their decision. It is estimated that considerable psychological turmoil is found in most adults for up to two years (Hetherington, 1988) before the decision to leave the marriage is taken. The fact that the legal side of the divorce process tends to be long-drawn-out does not facilitate this, but the psychological adjustments involved also take time. Many people are confronting a total change in lifestyle, along with the separation from their partner, all of which places severe demands on their psychological resources.

ADULTS: LONG-TERM EFFECTS

Although the period of intense disturbance after divorce tends to last for only a year or two in most cases, a substantial minority of people will never totally recover their former equilibrium (Hetherington, 1989). Wallerstein and Blakeslee (1989) report that five years after divorce the majority of adults in their sample 'felt they were better off, but a surprisingly large number did not. Half the men and two thirds of the women were more content with the quality of their lives. The rest, however, were either at a standstill or felt more troubled and unhappy than they had during the marriage.'

Life post-divorce can take a variety of different paths: many people re-marry – in the USA 80 per cent of divorced men and 75 per cent of divorced women – and of these, some will divorce and marry again, whereas some people never find another partner after their divorce. Children and step-children create more permutations, all of which militate the likelihood of a final common outcome.

Life post-divorce tends to be very different for men and women. Those men who do not find another stable partnership may be at particular risk of isolation and loneliness, since men are often less able than women to establish strong kinship and social networks. Although more petitions for divorce are brought by women (71 per cent in the UK in 1984, according to Burgoyne, Ormrod and Richards, 1987) most women end up poorer than before (Weitzman, 1985). This consequence is of course not specific to divorce. As Ward (1993) comments in relation to the Irish situation: 'It is simply wrong to state that divorce, of itself, causes poverty for women and children…the financial crisis heralded by separation is…an established feature of our society'. Over 90 per cent of women will have the main responsibility for the children. Coping with relative poverty and a general reduction in quality of life is stressful. Taking on a new full-time job, if such is available or feasible given the lack of child-care facilities, and coping alone with children can leave women both lonely and exhausted (Kelly, 1982). It is here that one can see a critical role for the state in ensuring that poverty is not the lot of the divorced woman and her family, and that women who wish to work are supported in doing so.

CHILDREN: SHORT-TERM EFFECTS

There is general agreement that most children will be distressed at some point in the divorce process, and that children who have experienced the breakdown of their parents' marriage will have more psychological problems than children whose parents claim to have happy marriages (Emery, 1988). Distress may have been evident in the child before the intention to divorce was made known to them, as they reacted to the problems in the marriage or to parental unhappiness, but in many cases the child might have been quite unaware of the existence of any threat to his or her family. The actual level of distress and disturbance found in children of intact families varies: for a difference on an outcome measure to be statistically significant it does not need to be large, nor does the discovery of statistically different differences imply that all children of divorced parents are less well adjusted than all children still living with both parents. It is of course possible that the extent of an individual child's distress is not being picked up by our current psychological assessment procedures.

Children's responses are highly dependent on their age. The young child's distress may be due to their sensitivity to their parents' distress and the change in their parents' attitudes and behaviours towards them. Parents under stress are rarely capable of parenting in a calm, consistent and sensitive fashion, no matter how good their intentions and how strong their attachment to their children (Hetherington, 1988). This will be the case for children of all ages, although lack of parental attention, consistency and sensitivity to the child's needs will have different consequences at later stages in development.

Young children may be devastated by the loss of a parental attachment figure, and become very fearful of losing the remaining parent. Grief at the loss of the non-custodial parent will also be experienced by the older child, but they will have a more sophisticated level of understanding of what is happening. They may well experience a great deal of anger, which can be directed at both parents, and they will often express their anger and distress in disobedient and defiant behaviour. None of this is helped by the parent's less than optimal capacity to provide good parenting.

Teenagers are inclined to express their anger and unhappiness by spending more time outside the family. Disengagement from the family may be accompanied by increased law-breaking and promiscuous sexual activity. In school, older children tend to have problems in school with both conduct and achievement. In many studies boys seem to show more evidence of persistent disturbance than girls, which may be due to their increased tendency to 'act out' when distressed, or to the effects of the departure of their father (Hetherington, 1989). However, Allison and Furstenberg (1989) did not find any such gender difference in their very large USA-based sample of children whose parents had divorced.

On the positive side, divorce may bring with it a therapeutic escape from family turmoil, and a number of researchers have commented on the high levels of maturity and competence seen in children who have weathered this crisis. Hetherington (1988) reports that, two years after the divorce, 'girls from divorced families were functioning well and had positive relationships with their custodial mothers'.

CHILDREN: LONG-TERM EFFECTS

In those countries where divorce has been studied over time, it has become clear that for quite a large number of children the divorce of their parents is the first stage in a prolonged series of familial transitions. After the divorce, children will have to adapt to life in a lone-parent household. For many this will be followed by the re-marriage of that parent, then perhaps by divorce and life in a lone-parent household once again.

Adjustment to step-parents, step-siblings and half-siblings all add complications to which children of different ages, gender and personalities will respond in different ways. Too much change and unpredictability is typically experienced as stressful for children (Garmezy and Rutter, 1983), and may be particularly bewildering for young children.

Recent reports from longitudinal studies have warned about the frequency of what have been termed 'sleeper effects'. There is evidence that some children who appear to cope well at the time of the divorce can start to have problems many years later. Several studies report that girls, who may not have shown much evidence of disturbance around the time of divorce, start to become rebellious and get into difficulties with sexual relationships in their teenage years (Wallerstein and Blakeslee, 1989; Hetherington, 1989). It should be borne in mind, however, that the problems which emerge later may not be directly caused by the divorce but by intervening circumstances, and that many of the well-known longitudinal studies do not have control groups of children from similar backgrounds who may well have had problems in the teenage or early adult years also.

There are now a number of studies of adults who have exerienced their parents' divorce, and these have been usefully reviewed by Amato and Keith (1991b). The express concern is that for some people who have experienced parental divorce, the eventual impact on their lives, as adults, may be more deleterious than the short-term emotional and social problems evident in childhood. Early studies reported that children of divorced parents were themselves more likely to divorce but, as divorce becomes more normative, this association is getting weaker (Burgoyne, Ormrod and Richards, 1987; Emery, 1988).

In relation to children's psychological wellbeing, it is important to remember that the break-up of their parents' marriage is just one of a range of potentially damaging events or circumstances to which children can be exposed. Intact families can be the cradles of neglect and abuse, whether physical, sexual or emotional, and do not guarantee children's safety and wellbeing. Furthermore, some children in very normal families will have problems which can not be put down to their parents' failings.

MINIMISING THE NEGATIVE CONSEQUENCES

Marital breakdown, like war or illness, is an intrinsically unwelcome and negative phenomenon. Many people will carry the scars of the breakdown of their own marriage or the breakdown of their parents' marriage with them for the rest of their days, but the likelihood is that for most people those marks are scars, not open wounds. Some may find themselves strengthened by having coped with this crisis, and feel more capable of dealing with other life adversities facing them. A minority will not find the personal resources or external supports needed to help them to recover.

Some level of marital breakdown among the population appears to be inevitable, but much more could be done to help marriages – including common-law marriages – survive and prosper. Unrealistic expectations of marriage and of the opposite sex might be less likely if marriage and relationships were recognised as important subjects for schoolchildren to learn about and discuss. Sex education and freely available contraception could help prevent rushed or early marriages. The presence of children can prevent marital breakdown, if parents resolve to stay together because of them, but it is also a cause of marriage breakdown when parents are poorly equipped for parenting and where, perhaps, illness or handicap in the child bring extra demands. Parents have little education or support for this role.

If marriages are in difficulty it should be possible for adults to turn to a state-funded marriage-guidance service for help. Parents contemplating ending their marriage need help to understand the effects of their actions and decisions on their children's wellbeing.

Children suffering the effects of their parents' marital turmoil should also have easy access to assistance. Teachers should be trained to recognise symptoms of distress and have the ready back-up of child-care professionals.

In all of these there should not be a rush to total dependency on professionals, but also a re-affirmation of a willingness on the part of the community in general to support relatives and friends who are in difficulty. If, despite the very best efforts of all involved, a marriage ends, mediation should be readily available to all couples. Parents should be advised on their children's needs, and the children's needs and rights and opinions on the proceedings should be taken fully into account in the divorce process. Garwood (1990) describes the benefits of the direct involvement of children in family-conciliation services in Scotland. Legislative changes, such as those facilitating the option of shared joint custody, may be an essential part of ensuring the best possible outcome in the circumstances, ie a conflict-free separation and, for the children of the marriage, continued contact with both parents, who are, despite all, working together in the best interests of their children.

Legislative changes will also be needed to improve the financial circumstances of lone parents and their children (Ward,

1993). Families do not live in vacuums. They are threatened by events and social changes occuring in the world around them. The psychological consequences of marital problems and marital breakdown could be seen, at one level, as being of concern only to those involved, but this is clearly an attitude which is unsustainable, being neither caring nor realistic. Problems and changes in marriage reflect problems and changes in society. Marital breakdown is a problem for the whole community. We, in Ireland, can choose to promote measures which will actively sustain families, and we can choose to promote measures which will minimise the psychological problems consequent on marital breakdown. It should not be a matter of supporting either marriage or divorce. The introduction of divorce may provide the stimulus needed for us, as a society and as a community, to take our responsibilities in relation to marriage and the family more seriously.

REFERENCES

Allison P D and Furstenberg J F, 'How marital dissolution affects children: variation by age and sex,' *Developmental Psychology*, 25, 540-550), 1989.

Amato, P R and Keith, B, 'Parental divorce and the well-being of children: a meta-analysis', *Psychological Bulletin*, 110, 26-46, 1991a.

Amato, P R and Keith, B, 'Parental divorce and adult wellbeing'. *Journal of Marriage and the Family*, 53, 43-58, 1991b.

Bilge, B and Kaufman G, 'Children of divorce and one-parent families: cross-cultural perspectives', *Family Relations*, 32, 59-71, 1983.

Block J, Block J H and Gerdje P F, 'The personality of children prior to divorce: a prospective study', *Child Development*, 57, 827-840, 1986.

Burgoyne J, Ormrod R and Richards M, *Divorce Matters*, Harmondsworth: Penguin, 1987

Clancy, P, 'Demographic changes in the Irish family' in 'The Changing Family', Dublin: Family Studies Unit (UCD), 1985.

Clingempeel W G and Segal S, 'Stepparent-stepchild relationships and the psychological adjustment of children in stepmother and stepfather families', *Child Development*, 59, 474-484, 1986.

Cummings E, Iannotti R and Zahn-Waxler C, 'The influence of conflict between adults on the emotions and aggression of young children', *Developmental Psychology*, 21, 495-507, 1985

Elliott J and Richards M, 'Children and divorce: educational performance and behaviour before and after parental separation', *International Journal of Law and the Family*, 5 258-276, 1991.

Emery R E, 'Interparental conflict and the children of discord and divorce', *Psychological Bulletin*, 92, 310-330, 1982.

Emery R E, *Marriage, Divorce and Children's Adjustment*, Newbury Park: Sage, 1988.

Fine-Davis M, *Changing gender role attitudes in Ireland 1975-86 Vol III:* Attitudes to moral issues in relation to voting behaviour in recent referenda. In Third Report of the Second Joint Committee on Women's Rights, 1988. Dublin: Stationery Office, 1988.

Garmezy N and Rutter M, *Stress, Coping and Development in Children*. New York: McGraw Hill, 1983.

Garwood F, 'Involving children in conciliation', *Children and Society*, 3, 311-324, 1990.

Hannan D, 'Changes in family relationship patterns', *Social Studies* 2, 559-565, 1973.

Hetherington E M, Cox M and Cox R, *Effects of Divorce on Parents and Children in Nontraditional Families*, M Lamb (Ed.) New Jersey: Lawrence Erlbaum, 1982.

Hetherington E M, *Parents, children and siblings: six years after divorce* in *Relationships within families*, R. Hinde and J. Stevenson-Hinde, 1988.

Hetherington E M, 'Coping with family transitions: winners, losers and survivors', *Child Development* 60 1-14, 1989.

Jeffers A and Fitzgerald M, *Families under Stress*, Vol. 2, Dublin: Eastern Health Board, 1991.

Kelly J B 'Divorce: the adult perspective'. In *Handbook of Developmental Psychology*, J Wolman (Ed.), New York: Prentice Hall, 1982.

McCullagh C, 'A tie that binds: family and ideology in Ireland', *Economic and Social Review*, 22 199-212, 1991

Rutter M and Rutter M, *Developing Minds*. Harmondsworth: Penguin, 1992.

Sheehan M F and Byrne J G, 'Review of two and a half years' admissions to a children's residential treatment unit', *Irish Journal of Psychiatry*, 10 8-12, 1982.

Wallerstein J S and Kelly J B, *Surviving the Breakup: How children and parents cope with divorce*. London: Grant McIntyre, 1980.

Wallerstein J. S. and Blakeslee S.: *Second Chance: men, women and children a decade after divorce*. Bantam Press, Uxbridge (1989).

Ward P, D*ivorce in Ireland: who should bear the cost?* Cork: Cork University Press, 1993.

Warshak R A and Santrock J W 'The impact of divorce in father-custody and mother-custody homes: the child's perspective'. In L A Kurdek (Ed.) *Children and Divorce*. San Francisco: Jossey Bass, 1983.

Weiss R, *Marital Separation*, New York: Basic Books, 1975.

Weitzman L J, *The Divorce Revolution*, New York:Free Press, 1985.

Legal Changes in the Law Covering Marital Breakdown in Ireland

Dervla Browne

Since the 1986 referendum there have been considerable changes in the law relating to marital breakdown in Ireland. The most important and far-reaching change has been the enactment of the Judicial Separation and Family Law Reform Act 1989 (hereafter referred to as the 1989 Act). Not only did this Act change the basis on which spouses can legally separate; it also introduced many new reliefs which may now be obtained once a decree of separation is granted.

There have been other changes since 1986. The Status of Children Act 1987 improves the legal position of the non-marital family. The Supreme Court has decided the basis on which a foreign divorce obtained before 1986 will be recognised in this country. There have been changes in the social-welfare law which have had a significant effect on the financial consequences of marital breakdown. The Matrimonial Homes Bill 1993, which proposed to change the law relating to ownership of the family home, was declared unconstitutional.

THE JUDICIAL SEPARATION AND FAMILY LAW REFORM ACT 1989

The Grounds

Prior to 19 October 1989 a husband or wife could obtain a judicial separation (or divorce a mensa et thoro as it was then called) only by proving that the other was guilty of cruelty, adultery or unnatural practices. The 1989 Act sets out that a decree of judicial separation may be granted on any of the following grounds:

- adultery;
- desertion for a period of in excess of a year prior to the date of the application;
- behaviour on the part of one spouse such that it is unreasonable to expect the other to continue to cohabit with her/him;

- lack of a normal marital relationship for a period in excess of a year;
- factual separation for a period of a year prior to applying to court and the other spouse consents to a separation;
- factual separation for more than three years prior to the date of applying to the court.

It appears from the White Paper on Marital Breakdown (1993) that the vast majority of decrees of judicial separation are granted on the 'no-fault' ground, ie on the lack of a normal marital relationship for over a year. This is the case even where one or more of the other grounds are pleaded. This is an obvious attempt by the courts to avoid ongoing hostility between the husband and the wife. The only problems arising from the use of this ground would appear to be in some cases where a wife seeks Deserted Wife's Allowance or Benefit. Queries have been raised by the Department of Social Welfare as to why a decree was not sought or obtained on the ground of desertion or unreasonable behaviour.

Even where any one of the grounds is shown to exist, the court may grant a decree only once it is satisfied that:

- the spouses have received advice about mediation and separation by agreement;
- proper provision has been made for the children of the marriage. If the court intends making orders to provide for the children, then it can grant the judicial separation.

In many cases the husband and the wife will have attended mediation but will have failed to reach agreement there. In almost all cases there will have been some attempt by the legal advisers to reach agreement on the terms of a separation. If these attempts are not successful there is no alternative but to proceed to a court hearing.

Orders regarding Property, Maintenance and Children
Once a decree of judicial separation is granted, the court has wide discretion to make other orders (called ancillary orders) to regulate the financial and other affairs of the separated spouses.

The 1989 Act provides for maintenance for the dependent spouse and/or children. This includes lump-sum payment and/or periodical maintenance. The maintenance can be secured in any manner which the court deems appropriate. The power to award lump-sum maintenance is a new and useful power, as under the Family Law (Maintenance of Spouses and Children) Act 1976, the court can award only periodic (ie weekly or monthly payments) maintenance. This is inadequate in the case of redundancy payments or where one spouse receives a lump sum, for example from a claim for compensation.

There is an obvious flaw in the 1989 Act in that a wife who does wish to separate or who is already separated by agreement cannot seek a lump-sum maintenance payment. She must apply under the Family Law (Maintenance of Spouses and Children) Act 1976. A wife who has applied to the court for a judicial separation and who obtains weekly maintenance may re-apply for a lump sum in the event that her husband becomes redundant. However, if the husband and wife separate by agreement and the weekly maintenance ceases because of redundancy, the wife does not appear to be able to apply for a lump sum. There is a welcome proposal in the Family Law Bill 1994 to change the law to allow the grant of lump sums under the Family Law (Maintenance of Spouses and Children) Act 1976.

The power given to the court by the 1989 Act to secure the maintenance payments gives a measure of protection to the spouses of self-employed persons. Under the 1976 Act the only means by which a wife could secure payment of maintenance was to have the husband's earnings attached – that is to receive the payment directly from the husband's employer. In the event that the husband is self-employed, there are no wages to attach. The 1989 Act enables the court to make orders securing the maintenance against other income available to a self-employed spouse or to secure the maintenance against property, eg the husband's share of the family home. The Family Law Bill 1994 proposes a change to the Family Law (Maintenance of Spouses and Children) Act 1976 to allow the court make secured payments.

The 1989 Act allows a spouse apply for lump sum or other form of maintenance any number of times once the decree is granted. This may give rise to problems for the paying spouse (usually the husband). The husband and the wife may wish to finally resolve their financial affairs, and the wife may agree to a lump sum instead of ongoing periodic maintenance. If both parties are independently advised and agree to this payment being a final settlement, then there seems to be no good reason why this sort of agreement should not be binding. However, the case of *HD-v-PD* (1978) is generally accepted as correctly stating the law relating to an agreement not to re-apply for maintenance under the 1976 Act. The dependent spouse cannot be legally bound by any such agreement. It would appear from the 1989 Act that this is also the case where the court orders a lump sum rather than periodic maintenance. This is no bar to the dependent spouse seeking further lump sums or periodic maintenance.

The 1989 Act provides that the court may direct one spouse to transfer any property to which s/he is entitled to the other, for the benefit of that spouse or the children. These orders are known as property-adjustment orders. They are most commonly sought in respect of the family home, where applications are made on the part of one spouse – for example, the wife – who is a non-owner to have the house transferred into the joint names of the spouses, or, in appropriate cases, to have the house transferred into her sole ownership.

This is an important change in the law, as it allows a spouse who has in no way contributed to the acquisition of the home to obtain a share in the property. It is not necessary for the wife to show that she has paid anything towards the acquisition of the home or other property. It can be sought in respect of any property owned by either spouse, as there is no concept of marital property in Irish law.

The 1989 Act puts the separating spouse in a better position than the spouse who is happily married. A spouse can apply for a property adjustment order only if s/he has obtained a decree of judicial separation. Otherwise the spouse who is not a legal owner must establish that s/he has contributed either directly or indirectly to the acquisition of the family home in order to obtain a share in it. This of course will be impossible to prove in certain cases – for example, where the family home is inherited by one of the spouses.

The Act specifically states that the court can consider and decide whether or not a property-adjustment order should be made on a single occasion only, unless there is wilful conceal-ment of material information on that occasion. Therefore, once an order is sought and either granted or refused, a spouse cannot re-apply for further orders in respect of any other property acquired or in the ownership of the other spouse.

This section is a clear attempt to introduce the notion of a final settlement, such as exists in the English divorce jurisdiction, into Irish law. However, in practice problems are likely to arise in respect of this provision. In many cases the court has ordered the transfer of property to a wife, for example by the transfer of the family home into her sole name, because the husband cannot afford to pay maintenance. The intention is that instead of weekly maintenance the wife receives a valuable asset from the husband. In the event that circumstances improve for the husband – for example if he obtains employment – there is no bar to the wife re-applying for maintenance even though she is now sole owner of the family home. However, the husband cannot seek a property-transfer order in respect of the house. One order is final and the other cannot be.

The other potential problem concerns a situation where the court refuses to grant a transfer of the family home to the wife on the basis that the husband will continue to be responsible for the mortgage repayments. If circumstances change – for example, if the husband ceases to pay the mortgage or maintenance – the wife cannot re-apply to have the home transferred into her name.

The court has power to make a number of other orders after granting a separation, including the declaration of interest in property. Such orders are described as follows.

The right of residence

The court can grant a right of residence in the family home to one spouse to the exclusion of the other for life, or other period as may be decided by the court.

Prior to the enactment of the 1989 Act, a spouse wishing to reside in the family home apart from the other spouse after sepa-ration had to show grounds – ie a threat to safety and welfare –

for a barring order. The criteria to be used in deciding which spouse is to occupy the family home is set out in the Act and has been interpreted in the case of *K-v-K* (1990).

The 1989 Act states that in deciding whether to order the sale of the house or to grant a right of residence to one spouse, the court has to take into account the fact that: (a) where a decree of judicial separation is granted it is not possible for the spouses to continue to reside together; and (b) that proper and secure accommodation should, where practicable, be provided for a dependent spouse and any dependent child of the family. This has been interpreted as requiring a court to exclude one spouse where the house is not to be sold or partitioned, or where a barring order is not granted.

Given the criteria as set out in the Act and as interpreted by the High Court, it is likely that where the house is not very valuable and there are dependent children, the spouse with custody will continue to reside in the family home. In low-income families this obviously operates to the disadvantage of husbands. However, as research in this country and elsewhere has shown, marital breakdown has an inevitable impoverishing effect, particularly on low-income families.

In the light of the operation of the 1989 Act, there must be a review of local-authority housing policy. When deciding what financial relief to grant after a divorce, the English courts have taken into account the fact that local-authority housing is available for the spouse with custody of the children.

The Barring or Protection Order
The 1989 Act also allows the court make a barring or protection order, but it is no longer necessary to seek this relief, and it is not sought unless there is violence or a real risk to the safety and health of the spouse and/or the children.

The Sale of the Family Home
The 1989 Act provides for the court to order the sale of the family home, and for its partition. In very rare circumstances the court may direct that the house is physically partitioned, so that it is converted into two independent residences. The family home may be sold if there are sufficient funds to rehouse the

dependent children and spouse in a suitable manner. Even in these circumstances the court may not wish to uproot dependent children, and the figures in the White Paper on Marital Breakdown show that in only 36 of 354 cases was the family home sold. In a childless marriage there is an increased possibility that the family home will be sold to allow the husband and the wife go their separate ways.

Custody and Access
The 1989 Act provides for the grant of orders regarding the children, ie custody, access and any other matters regarding their welfare.

Succession Rights
The Act gives the court discretion to extinguish one or both of the spouses' succession rights, and the extinguishing of both spouses' succession rights has become usual. This does not affect the rights of the children in the estate of either parent.

The criteria to be applied by the court in deciding what financial orders to make are as follows:

- the income, earning capacity, property and other financial resources which each of the spouses has or is likely to have in the foreseeable future;
- the financial needs, obligation and responsibilities which each of the spouses has, or is likely to have in the foreseeable future;
- the standard of living enjoyed by the family before separation or proceedings;
- the age of the spouses, the length of the marriage and the time they lived together;
- any physical or mental disability of either spouse;
- the contributions which each spouse has made, or is likely to make in the foreseeable future, to the welfare of the family, including the contribution made by each to the income-earning capacity, property and financial resources of the other, and any contributions by looking after the family;
- the effect on the earning capacity of each spouse of the marital responsibilities assumed by each;

- any income or benefits to which either spouse is entitled by or under the statute
- the conduct of each of the spouses if that conduct is such that, in the opinion of the court it would, in all circumstances be repugnant to justice to disregard the accommodation needs of either spouse.

The Irish law draws heavily on the English Matrimonial and Family Law Proceedings Act 1984, which will be discussed in the next chapter. It is based on the principle of fair rather than equal distribution. A wide discretion is given to the court to divide the assets of the spouses in such manner as is fair and reasonable. The court can take into account and can make orders in respect of all assets of the spouses, and not just those assets acquired during the marriage. There are scant judicial guidelines as to the weight to be attached to any one of these factors. It would appear that the relative needs of both spouses is the primary factor.

Summary
The Judicial Separation and Family Law Reform Act 1989 has put in place a procedure whereby all matters arising in a separation my be dealt with by a court in the event that they cannot be agreed. A number of features stand out in the present operation of the Act.

- the amount of discretion given to the judiciary and lack of statutory or judicial guide-lines. The lack of judicial guide-lines is mainly due to the fact that all but a few cases are dealt with by the Circuit Court, which does not usually deliver written judgments and which does not create precedent.
- The emphasis on retaining the family home as a residence for the wife and children where there is little equity in the house and where the children are dependent.
- The assumption which underlies the Irish system that maintenance of a spouse is a lifelong obligation.
- The lack of emphasis on encouraging a dependent spouse to become self-sufficient.

THE CONSTITUTIONAL CHALLENGE

In 1994, in the case of *F-v-F, Ireland and the Attorney General* (1994), it was argued that the 1989 Act was unconstitutional for the following reasons:

- the discretion of the court to grant a decree of judicial separation on the grounds that there had not been a normal marital relationship between the spouses was unconstitutional in that it enabled a spouse to obtain a separation where the other spouse was blameless and did not consent. This, it was argued, could lead to disastrous consequences for the spouse who did not wish to be separated in that his property rights and right to family life could be seriously curtailed as a result of the separation;
- the court's power to grant an exclusion order was an interference in the property rights of a spouse who owned the property but who was excluded from enjoyment of it.

On 28 July 1994, the High Court declared that the Act was constitutional. The Court found:

- that the grant of a decree on the grounds that the marriage had broken down to such a degree that no normal marital relationship had existed between the parties for over a year was little more than an official recognition of an existing state of affairs and an attempt by the legislature to allow for an appropriate resolution of affairs between the spouses; and
- that the grant of an exclusion order did not constitute an attack on property rights of one party, as it was an attempt to provide for both spouses and the children in a situation where the marriage had broken down.

FAMILY LAW BILL 1994

One of the primary aims of the Family Law Bill 1994 is to allow those parties to a marriage which has been declared null and void claim the relief available to separated spouses and, in some cases, to claim relief which is not available to separated spouses. Persons who have succeeded in obtaining a decree of nullity are able legally to remarry in Ireland, as the court has found that their first marriage ceremony was not valid. It appears from the Bill that the intention is to treat these persons in the same manner as (and in some cases more favourably than) those who are validly married but who now seek a separation.

While it is clear that some financial relief should be available for those whose marriages are declared void, it is not appropriate that they should be dealt with in the same manner as those whose relationship has the benefit of constitutional protection. It seems obvious that the appropriate solution is to allow spouses apply for a divorce and suitable financial relief, rather than encourage people to pursue the often artificial remedy of nullity in order to achieve the desired result, namely the ability legally to remarry. The experience in England has been that the remedy of nullity is rarely used once divorce was made available.

The Bill contains other proposals to reform the 1989 Act. For example, it is proposed to allow spouses apply and re-apply for property-adjustment orders, or to vary existing orders. This proposal is clearly undesirable, as it leads to continuing litigation and makes it impossible to allow spouses to settle their financial affairs once and for all. However, there is a need to allow review of these orders in limited circumstances: for example, where there was no order made on the basis that the husband would continue to pay the mortgage but has not done so, or on the basis that the house was in satisfaction of the husband's liability to maintain and the wife had now sought maintenance (or the Department of Social Welfare has sought a contribution from the husband).

The Bill makes it easier to enforce maintenance orders and gives the court power to make lump-sum orders on an interim basis.

Reforms of the 1989 Act which are necessary but not proposed in the 1994 Bill include that of giving the court power to direct that one spouse provides a life policy for the benefit of the other, clarifying the grounds on which ancillary orders are to be made, and providing statutory protection of the family home against debt.

RECOGNITION OF FOREIGN DIVORCES

The law regarding the recognition of foreign divorces was changed by the 1986 Domicile and Recognition of Foreign Divorces Act. This states that any divorce granted after 2 October 1986 will be recognised in Ireland if either of the spouses is domiciled in the foreign country where the divorce is granted. Domicile means that the person lives in the country and intends to live there indefinitely.

The decision of the Supreme Court in *W-v-W* (1993) had the effect that foreign divorces granted before 1986 are recognised in Ireland if granted in a country where either of the spouses is domiciled.

The fact that certain foreign divorces can be recognised in this country leads to considerable confusion. A wife whose husband's English divorce is recognised in Ireland is no longer a spouse for the purpose of applying for maintenance or a barring order, or for the purposes of the Succession Act 1965.

In many cases it is difficult to ascertain where one of the spouses is domiciled. Many people who have obtained foreign divorces are not sure that these divorces are recognised in Ireland. These people live in a state of limbo, not knowing whether they can re-marry, or whether they are entitled to reliefs or remedies available only to married persons.

The status of those whose foreign divorces are recognised here has been dealt with to some extent by the Family Law Bill 1994. That Bill proposes to allow persons who are divorced in another jurisdiction to apply for maintenance and other orders once certain conditions are satisfied. In the event that divorce is made available in this jurisdiction, this problem will be to some extent ameliorated, as fewer foreign applications will be made.

THE STATUS OF CHILDREN ACT 1987

This Act introduced the following changes in the legal status of children born outside marriage:

- the concept of illegitimacy was abolished;
- children born outside marriage have the same inheritance rights and rights to be maintained by their parents as children born in marriage;

- the procedure for applying for maintenance is now the same as if the child was born within marriage;
- it is possible for a person born outside marriage to obtain a declaration of parentage declaring a named person to be his or her parent;
- the court may order blood tests to determine parentage in any case where the issue is raised;
- the natural father of a child may apply to be appointed a guardian of the child.

However, the family outside marriage and in particular those in second unions are still unprotected. A cohabitee cannot apply for a barring order in the event of violent behaviour by her partner. The cohabitee cannot seek maintenance for herself. She has no rights to inherit from her partner's estate. She has no right in respect of any property other than that which she legally owns or to which she has contributed. Although she cannot claim maintenance from her cohabitee, she is unable to claim lone parent's allowance because she is cohabiting.

There is a clear case to be made for permitting those in second relationships to remarry and thereby achieve the legal status which reflects the reality of their relationship.

THE MATRIMONIAL HOMES BILL 1993

In 1993 the Matrimonial Homes Bill proposed to amend the law in respect of ownership of the family home. Irish law is based on the principle that ownership of property even in marriage depends on legal title or contribution. This means that if a spouse is on the title of property s/he will be presumed to own it, and if he or she is not the legal owner, s/he can establish an interest in it by showing that s/he contributed to its acquisition either directly or indirectly.

The Bill sought to introduce in a limited way the notion of community property. This notion is based on the principle that property acquired during marriage by either or both spouses belongs to both in equal shares. The Bill dealt only with the matrimonial home and provided that all existing or future matrimonial homes belong to both spouses as joint owners. The legal effect of this provision would be that where one spouse dies, the other becomes sole owner of the home. The Bill allowed married couples or intending married couples to agree that the Bill would not apply to their home. This would have been a significant change in the law and may have encouraged the practice of couples entering into pre-nuptial agreements to regulate their matrimonial affairs.

The difficulty which may have been encountered by the introduction of this legislation is that met in Californian law. The notion of equality tended to inhibit the judiciary, preventing the granting of more than one half of the share of the matrimonial assets to one of the spouses on divorce. The other problem was that of debt. If one spouse, for example the husband, ran up debts which could be registered against the family home, the wife is protected if the home is in her name or if she shows that she paid for it. If the house is automatically in joint names, then the debt may be registered against the husband's share, and this may result in the family home being sold to satisfy the debt.

The Matrimonial Homes Bill 1993 was referred to the Supreme Court for a decision as to its constitutionality. On 24 January 1994 the Supreme Court found that the Bill was repugnant to the Constitution. (1994 1ILRM 241) The Supreme Court found that the Bill constituted an interference with the authority of the family to decide how and by whom the family home should be owned.

SOCIAL WELFARE

There have been two primary social-welfare changes in recent years. First, the State introduced a new means-tested payment, namely the Lone Parents Allowance, which replaces the Unmarried Mother's Allowance, Deserted Husband's Allowance and the Widower's Non-Contributory Pension. In all cases where a single parent has dependent children living with her/him s/he can apply for Lone Parent's Allowance. The Deserted Wives' benefit is still payable as there is no Social Insurance payment for lone parents.

The second important change in the legislation has been to enable the Department of Social Welfare to recover contributions from a liable relative (whether a deserting spouse or the absent parent) towards the support of a recipient of Lone Parent's

Allowance, Deserted Wives' Benefit or allowance, or the Supplementary Welfare allowance. Any monies received by the recipient on foot of a maintenance order must be transferred to the Department of Social Welfare or the Department of Health. This has had the effect that women in receipt of the relevant social-welfare payments lose the benefit of any maintenance order if the order is less than the social-welfare payment.

The judiciary must be made aware of social-welfare changes and legislation as in many cases the wife's social-welfare payments are regarded as income in deciding the husband's liability to pay.

The changes have created a poverty trap for low-income families, where, for example, the husband cannot afford to pay any more than a nominal sum of maintenance. Even so, this extra income of, say, £10 or £20 per week will allow the wife and children some margin of security. The present legislation does not permit the wife or children to keep the payment, the effect being that the wife and children are no better off and the husband loses £10 or £20 of his income to the state. Once again it is the low-income family that suffers.

The other problem is similar to that which has beset the Child Support Agency in England. In many cases the court may order, or the parties agree, that as the husband's income is so low, he will not be required to pay maintenance but instead will be required to transfer the home to the wife's sole name. This agreement or order does not bind the Department of Social Welfare, and the husband is still liable to assessment and enforced payment of a contribution to the Department or to the wife. As the property-adjustment order is final, it cannot be reviewed or varied. This is an obviously unfair outcome and must be tackled by change in the social-welfare scheme.

PROPOSED CHANGES

The White Paper on Marital Breakdown provides for a number of changes in the law relating to marital breakdown. Most importantly, it recommends that the constitutional ban on divorce be removed.

The report gives a number of options for the wording of the constitutional amendment. There are two general approaches.

The first is to pass an amendment allowing the Oireachtas enact law providing for the grant of a dissolution of marriage, and to leave it entirely to the Oireachtas to set out the grounds.

The second approach is to limit the grounds on which a divorce can be grounded by the wording of Article 41 – in other words, to retain a qualified ban on divorce.

The Report sets out different examples as to how this ban may be worded – for example one proposal is to state in the Constitution that the law can allow the court to grant a divorce only where there has not been a normal marital relationship for at least five years and where there is no hope of reconciliation. This would mean that there would continue to be a constitutional ban on divorce in all other circumstances.

The difficulties with the second approach is that in the event of another proposed change in the grounds for divorce the constitution will have to be amended. This has been shown to be unsatisfactory in the case of the pro-life debate which necessitated two amendments. The Irish people must have trust in the elected representatives.

The first approach would seem to be more appropriate. The people of Ireland should decide whether or not there should continue to be a ban on divorce, and if they decide that divorce should be permitted in Ireland, then it is a matter for the Oireachtas to introduce appropriate legislation.

The arguments for and against divorce have been rehearsed many times over the past decade, and they are outside the scope of these chapters. Other chapters in this book are based on an assumed consensus that there should be divorce in Ireland. The fundamental issues to be then addressed are those relating to:

- the grounds on which divorce should be granted; and
- the objective and aims of the financial reliefs available after divorce.

Dervla Browne

REFERENCES

White Paper on Marital Breakdown – a Review and Proposed Changes (1992). Including Irish Draft Family Law (No.2). Government Publications.

H D-v-P D Supreme Court, 8 May 1978, unreported.

K-v-K, Barron J., 25 October 1990, unreported.

F-v-F, Ireland and the Attorney General, High Court, 28 July 1994, unreported.

W-v-W, 1993 2I.R. 476.

In re article 25 of the Constitution and in re Matrimonial Homes Bill 1993 1994 1 ILRM 241.

Divorce in Other Jurisdictions
Including an overview of the White Paper

Dervla Browne

Having looked at the present law relating to marital breakdown, it is necessary to examine the proposed reforms contained in the White Paper on Marital Breakdown, with reference to research and reform in other countries. This paper is sadly lacking in information about ongoing change in divorce laws elsewhere. Given this dearth of information, it is hard to generate relevant or educated debate about divorce.

In the event that divorce is introduced in Ireland a unique opportunity will be presented to the Oireachtas to reform our family-law system. There are three particular challenges which face the government:

- to provide for the termination of marriage in a manner designed to prevent recrimination and facilitate amicable relations;
- to address successfully the question of the financial consequences of marital breakdown;
- to introduce law which adequately reflects the need to provide (both financially and emotionally) for the children of broken marriages.

THE GROUNDS FOR DIVORCE
The grounds on which divorce should be available is obviously a highly controversial issue. Should should proof of matrimonial misconduct be necessary?

The White Paper on Marital Breakdown proposes a draft Bill which includes four options as to the grounds on which divorce could be granted.

Option A requires proof of matrimonial misconduct such as adultery, unreasonable behaviour, or desertion for three years. There are also no-fault grounds, namely (B) factual separation for more than three years and both spouses consent; (C) factual separation for more than five years; (D) lack of a normal marital relationship for either three or five years. In all cases there must be no reasonable possibility of reconciliation.

Options B and C are strict no-fault grounds. Option B allows divorce where there has not been a normal marital relationship between the spouses for a period of five years, and where there is no hope of reconciliation. Option C states that divorce should be granted when the spouses have lived apart for more than five years and where there is no reasonable possibility of cohabitation being resumed.

Option D permits divorce where the spouses already have a judicial separation for two years. If they do not have a judicial separation, they can still obtain a divorce if the court is satisfied that they had grounds for a judicial separation two years before applying for a divorce. This option is inspired by the law in many European countries which require the the parties to separate before applying for a divorce.

Recent world trends have been towards a liberalisation of the grounds upon which a divorce is granted. Almost all USA states have moved towards no-fault divorce. Countries which provided for no-fault grounds, but which required proof of a lengthy period of time during which the spouses lived apart, have moved to shorten the period. The English legislation, which provided for both no-fault and fault grounds, has recently been the subject of review and there is now a proposal to reform the law to allow divorce, even where the other spouse does not consent, on the grounds of irretrievable breakdown. Breakdown is to be proved by the expiry of a fixed minimum of one year.

Swedish law reform acknowledges the right of one spouse to terminate the marriage at will. It does not refer to irretrievable breakdown.

The reasons for the need to change to no-fault divorce are identified by the English Law Reform Commission (Law Comm.170) as the problems inherent in the proof of bad behaviour, and the bitterness and hostility associated with the use of the fault grounds. At divorce or separation, there is a need to concentrate the minds of separating spouses on the financial consequences and the needs of the children. The rehearsal of allegations of adultery or other bad behaviour detracts from the real issues. Generally speaking, the requirement to prove fault leads to a hostile divorce which interferes with parenting of the children after separation or divorce.

It is accepted that in England, where, as we have seen, there are fault and no-fault grounds for divorce, the rules are abused. Rather than waiting for the two years necessary for divorce by consent, one spouse will agree to the other obtaining a divorce on the grounds of adultery, thus allowing an immediate divorce.

Option B and C, which require proof of breakdown of a marriage (that there has been no normal marital relationship for three or five years) would result in many spouses living in an intolerable situation for three or five years.

It is important to stress that at present a spouse can obtain a judicial separation if s/he gives evidence that the marriage has not been a normal one for over a year. There is in reality little defence to a judicial separation on these grounds, because if one partner is definite that the marriage has been a bad experience little can be said to contradict this. Can this spouse be forced to remain living with the other partner even though s/he is firmly of the view that the marriage is over?

It also seems to be a useless exercise to expect spouses to live separate and apart for five years when the marriage is obviously over. Divorce should not be about attempting to revive a dead marriage. The obligation to apply for a separation first is to allow for a period of reconsideration. Rather than make this extended period a requirement for divorce, it seems preferable to introduce a two-stage divorce that would allow some period of reconsideration before the divorce is made final.

Option D, as worded, is unsatisfactory. It requires the court to investigate whether grounds for a judicial separation existed at least two years before to the date of the hearing, something which will be most difficult to prove. It does not refer to those spouses already separated by separation agreement or by decree of divorce a mensa et thoro (the remedy which existed before the 1989 Judicial Separations Act), who should also be automatically entitled to a divorce if this provision were made law.

No-fault divorce is not ideal, however: its problems are these:

- it allows one party to repudiate the marriage, or effectively to terminate it, without matrimonial misconduct or consent of the other;

- it removes from the ambit of the court all issues as to conduct within the marriage and confines the issue to one of whether or not the marriage has broken down. The problem lies with the fact that the applying spouse can rely on his/her own behaviour – for example a husband can rely on his own adultery to establish that the marital relationship has not been normal. Once this ground is established then the wife is forced into a situation where her marriage is terminated, even though this may result in a worsening of her own economic situation. However, as Murphy J. found in the context of the Judicial Separation and Family Law Reform Act 1989, the grant of a decree of judicial separation on the grounds that there has not been a normal marital relationship is only making official a tragic reality. Once we decide that parties to an unsuccessful marriage should be allowed to remarry, is there any point in refusing that relief to a spouse who has had no relationship with the other for a substantial period of time, merely because the other spouse does not want the opportunity to remarry?;
- no-fault divorce has been found to weaken the bargaining position of the parties. The present English system which allows the non-consenting spouse delay or, in the case of financial hardship, deny the divorce, strengthens his or her bargaining power in respect of the financial reliefs. In other words, the wife who does not consent to a divorce may eventually do so if it is agreed that she gets the family home. This highlights a problem with the financial orders available after divorce. Women should be in an equal bargaining position in respect of finance and children, and should not have to resort to the tactic of opposing the divorce to ensure proper provision once it is granted. Reform of the law governing the distribution of assets and support is required, not the retention or introduction of divorce based on fault;
- the third problem is obvious even from the operation of the 1989 Judicial Separations Act. A spouse who wishes the court to hear about the other's misconduct must be told that, as there is no opposition to a separation on the grounds of lack of a normal marital relationship, it is doubtful that the court will wish to hear evidence about misconduct. Of course conduct is relevant where, for example, a spouse is seeking a

barring order. It will also be important where one of the spouses has gambled or otherwise disposed of family assets. There is a strong argument for the provision of a forum to allow a spouse to air his or her grievance about the cause of the marital breakdown. However, the courtroom is not the place, and therefore serious consideration should be given to an intervention programme or some form of counselling before divorce so that anger and grief can be resolved.

The primary argument against divorce and therefore against liberal divorce is that it weakens the structure of the family. This ignores the real issue. It is not the availability of divorce which weakens the family structure, but rather the lack of support structures for families and particularly those families with children. Many commentators have identified the need to educate for marriage and relationships at school, and to provide more family counselling, together with better economic protection in social welfare and tax for the family. Once a marriage fails, the law must provide a dignified means to allow the spouses terminate their marriage. No-fault divorce appears to be the only solution. If one spouse feels that the marriage is over and that there is no chance of reconciliation after a period of consideration, the law should respect this decision.

The White Paper fails to address currently raging English debate as to whether there should be fault or no-fault divorce. It does not propose any more liberal grounds for divorce than the lack of a normal marital relationship for three or five years. It does not refer to empirical evidence and proposed reform relating to fault or no-fault divorce in other countries. Unless this material is made widely available the pending Irish debate will be ill informed and any proposals incomplete.

The Irish draft Family Law (No. 2) Bill gives courts a discretion in cases where the application for divorce is grounded on no-fault grounds. The court can refuse to grant a divorce on these grounds if the divorce would result in grave financial or other hardship to the non-consenting spouse. The equivalent English law has been found to give women a bargaining weapon in negotiating settlements. The purpose of this section is stated in the White Paper as being to protect older wives who may lose succession rights or pension rights on divorce. It must be remembered that no such defence exists under the 1989 Act. Therefore, under the existing law, a husband may obtain a separation and seek and obtain any ancillary reliefs, such as the extinguishing of succession rights or the forced sale of a home, in the judicial separation proceedings. There is no statutory defence available to the older wife to argue that she will suffer hardship as a result of this application.

The most commonly cited example of financial hardship after divorce is the loss of pension rights. The White Paper specifically mentions this as being a loss which is not at present suffered by wives after separation – on the grounds that because they remain technically married they are still entitled to benefit. This is not necessarily the case, however, as under many pension schemes payment is made to a named beneficiary and not necessarily the spouse. This is not the only hardship suffered by spouses on separation. In practice, separation in low-income families has an adverse effect on both the husband and the wife. Where there are dependent children and very little equity in the home, the likelihood is that the husband will be ordered to leave while being obliged to pay maintenance or the mortgage while living away from the family home. In certain cases the spouses cannot afford to live apart and one or both will be caused great financial hardship.

These are fundamental economic consequences of marital breakdown, whether or not divorce is available. It is not enough to propose that a person be denied a divorce on the basis of financial hardship. The issue of loss of pension rights and issues as to poverty and continued parenting must be realistically addressed by legislation, and not side-stepped by allowing the courts refuse to grant a decree on these grounds.

ANCILLARY ORDERS

Marital breakdown and poverty
There is no doubt that marital breakdown has universally been found to cause poverty amongst women and children. In the constitutional debate in 1986 this was an argument which was used to great effect by the anti-divorce lobby, who made much use of American research and particularly Weitzman's 1985

survey of divorce in California. This showed a dramatic decline – of 70 per cent – in the living standards of women (and their children) in the year after divorce, and a 40 per cent rise in the living standards of divorced men in the same period. Only 13 per cent of women with children under six years old were awarded alimony. Only one in three older women obtained spousal support.

Reports from Canada and surveys in England and Australia all tell the same story of impoverishment resulting from separation and divorce. (Ekelaar and Maclean: 1986) A 1986 English study showed that only 18 per cent of women living alone with children after divorce were found to be living above 140 per cent of the supplementary welfare rate available. In Canada a 1990 report found that impoverishment of women and children was one of the major consequences of separation and divorce. Sixty-six per cent of women with child custody had total income, including support, at a level well below the poverty line. The consequence of separation for families in low income brackets is a worsening of economic circumstances.

It was this argument which dominated the debate about divorce in 1986 (Binchy). It was vehemently argued that, without divorce, women and children are protected by the law. Pro-divorce lobbies counter-argued that it was marital breakdown rather than divorce which caused poverty. In the absence of statistics to support it, this argument did not convince: statistics were available from other jurisdictions to show the effect of divorce, but none were available to show the effects of marital breakdown in Ireland.

Since 1986 some research has been carried out in this area and the figures speak for themselves. Sixty per cent of maintenance awards made in the District Court were for amounts less than the basic rate of Supplementary Allowance. In 81 per cent of cases, the amount was less than the maximum personal rate of Deserted Wife's Benefit. In other words, women would be better off on social welfare than in receipt of the maintenance awarded. Only nine per cent of orders were fully paid up on the date of the survey, and 64 per cent were in arrears. (Ward: 1993)

It is now an incontrovertible fact that in 'divorce-free' Ireland, families are suffering the same economic effects as a result of marriage breakdown as those suffered by families in other countries after divorce. Divorce does not cause poverty; on the contrary, divorce legislation, if properly drafted, can alleviate it.

The challenge is to address this problem in any proposed divorce legislation. We have available to us the experience in other countries, where over the past decade the law has been subject to ongoing debate and reform. The Irish legislature must identify the rationale and aim of any divorce legislation and must ground this rationale in empirical research in this country and comparative studies of the divorce regime in other countries.

The proposed Irish Family Law (No 2) Bill provides that, after divorce, a former spouse can apply for property orders at present available under the Judicial Separation and Family Law Reform Act 1989. The criteria to be applied in the case of divorce are effectively the same as those already existing under the 1989 Act, and have been set out in the preceding chapter.

This provision ignores the lessons learned in other countries. The Paper also fails to refer to important issues identified and addressed in other jurisdiction. These will be now be discussed.

MAINTENANCE AND SELF-SUFFICIENCY

During the 1980s the American legislation as regards alimony (maintenance) tended to encourage self-sufficiency of the dependent spouse (usually the wife). Most states listed a number of factors (similar to those matters listed in the 1989 Judicial Separation Act) to be considered by the court when deciding whether to award alimony; in practice, however, it was found that courts paid more attention to the wife's ability to be self-sufficient than to any other factor. Transitional payments or limited-time payments were common, the aim being to allow the wife time to re-educate herself and re-establish herself in the job market. Several states had a fixed time limit on all alimony awards.

Weitzman's 1985 study of Californian law showed that, despite legislative guarantees for the support for the three most vulnerable groups of women – mothers with young children, older women incapable of self-sufficiency and women who need help with transition – maintenance of the spouse was considered by the judiciary in nearly all cases to have the objective of making the spouse self-sufficient. The awards failed to take into account the devastating effect of child-bearing on the economic status of the wife.

In Canada (Bailey and Bala: 1990), a 1990 Government report found that the low income level of divorced families resulted from the increasingly low level of judicial orders for spousal support. Again the rationale determining the basis for support varied among family judges. Self-sufficiency appeared from some research to be the most common basis on which spousal support was granted. The report found that child-support payments were generally considered to be too low, with the financial burden falling mainly on the shoulders of the custodial parent, normally the wife. It would appear that Canadian family-law experts now favour the introduction of further statutory guidelines for the award of spousal and child support.

The English Law Reform Commission had in its 1980 report stated the primary principles in awarding financial relief to be the following:

- provision for the welfare of the children should be the primary objective;
- greater weight should be given to the importance of each party doing all possible to become self-sufficient;
- the clean-break principle is desirable wherever possible.

The factors which must now be taken into account in awarding maintenance and other financial relief are set out in the the 1984 Matrimonial and Family Proceedings Act, and they are similar to those listed in the Irish 1989 Judicial Separations Act: income, needs, standard of living, age and length of marriage, disability, contributions to the welfare of the family, conduct if unfair to ignore it are all to be taken into account. Further, the English 1984 Act specifies that the court should consider the value to either party of any benefit which s/he cannot now acquire as a result of the divorce.

Reviews of case law suggest, however, that there is no consistency in the application of these principles by the courts. There was a tendency for courts to order limited-time maintenance payments with the aim of re-establishing the dependent spouse in the marketplace.

The Scottish legislation (1990) provides that a party who has been dependent to a substantial degree on the financial support of the other spouse should be awarded such financial provision as is reasonable to enable him/her to adjust over a period of not more that three years from the date of the divorce. A party who, at the time of the divorce, seems likely to suffer serious financial hardship as a result of the divorce should be awarded such financial provision as is reasonable to relieve him/her of hardship over a reasonable period. The obvious intention is to re-establish the dependent spouse in the workplace, but the court can take into account relevant factors such as the age, health et cetera of the dependent spouse.

The problems associated with maintenance awarded on the basis of encouraging self-sufficiency were highlighted in the Weitzman survey and surveys in many other states. Women cannot easily re-establish themselves in the marketplace and, if they do, their earnings are generally lower than those of men.

A 1984 comparative study by Weitzman, prior to the change in the English law, found the operation of the English legislation to be more favourable to women, in that the judiciary were more paternalistic and that there tended to be an underlying assumption that the obligation to maintain a wife survived divorce.

It appears that a system based on a notion of self-sufficiency causes hardship for the following women:

- women with young children;
- older women who have been married and dependent for most of their lives;
- women in a state of transition from being dependent to re-entering the market place.

As a result of Weitzman's research and findings, a Task Force was set up in California and the law there has been reformed as follows:

- there is now a presumption of permanent support for dependent spouses in a marriage of long duration;
- support awards in marriages of long duration must have as their objective the equalising of standards of living of both households after divorce;

- in marriages other than those of long duration, the intent is to maintain the spouses and children to the standard to which they were maintained before divorce.
- there is now (since 1986) mandatory education of judges about gender bias and divorce.

The affects of these reforms are not yet known.

The difficulty with giving the judiciary the discretion which is proposed in the Irish White Paper is that the courts may place too much emphasis on a single factor – for example, self-sufficiency – causing the Irish courts to run into the same problems encountered in other jurisdictions.

CLEAN BREAK AND DIVISION OF ASSETS

The proposed Family Law Bill providing for divorce will allow the court make as many property-transfer orders about any property as it wishes at any time after the divorce. The principles to be applied are those of fair distribution. However, there have been problems with this type of division in other countries.

The American states differ in their approach to property division on marriage. Some states have a *community property system*, based on the notion that all property accumulated by the spouses during marriage (other than by gift or inheritance) is owned jointly. Other states have a *separate property system*, based on the notion that each spouse owns what he or she has acquired. This is the system currently existing in Ireland.

On divorce, the separate-property states generally allow the court to decide on an equitable (fair) distribution of the spouses' property. In some of these states the court can direct a transfer only of a share of the property acquired during marriage. The experience during the early 1980s was that this generally meant that a wife was given one third of the property.

In the community-property states, the legislation provides for an equal division of the marital property. This can lead to difficulties. Frequently the courts interpret the equal division of assets as demanding that the family home be sold after divorce in order that the assets be divided. Weitzman's 1985 Californian survey identified this tendency as one of the major causes of poverty after divorce. Further, there was marked reluctance on the part of the judiciary to award any more than half of the property to a spouse. The study showed that the older woman who had cared for now adult children, and the woman with young children, were most affected by orders for the sale of the family home.

In contrast, in her 1984 comparative survey, Weitzman found that there was a marked reluctance among the English judiciary to order the sale of the family home where this was the sole asset. However, under the English system (which was based on the notion of equitable or fair distribution) the wife was unlikely to obtain more than one third of the total assets of the marriage.

The principle of a clean break was given statutory authority in England in the Matrimonial and Family Proceedings Act 1984. The court now has a duty to decide in every case whether or not a clean break can be imposed.

The clean-break principle works well well in cases where there are sufficient assets to allow division in such a way that the spouse who has been disadvantaged or dependent receives a greater share. Where there is substantial capital there is no objection to achieving a clean break. Indeed, where both parties are independent, periodical maintenance seems irrelevant.

The difficulty arises in cases where there are very little assets and the possibility of a clean break depends on the dependent spouse's ability to earn. There is clearly a case to be made for a continuing maintenance obligation to a spouse in these circumstances. In England there is now pressure to reform the law for reimbursement or compensatory maintenance. In other words, if there are not enough assets available for fair or equitable distribution, but the husband has greater earning potential or is now in a position to pursue a career, the court can calculate the wife's contribution to this advancement and award an allowance or support on this basis. This moves away from the concept of dependency and into the area of ordinary debt arising from a partnership, and also takes into account a new form of property – 'career assets'. This is a revolutionary concept which could have beneficial effects for women.

Though it does not address or refer to it in any way, the Irish White Paper clearly rejects the notion of a clean break. It does so in five ways:

- the proposed Family Law (No. 2) Bill allows a former spouse to re-apply for a property adjustment order even though s/he has applied and obtained one in judicial separation proceedings;
- the Bill allows a party apply on any number of occasions to court for a property-adjustment order.
- the Bill makes no attempt to amend the existing law that a spouse cannot waive maintenance.
- the Bill does not mention those spouses separated by agreement in which all property has been divided and waivers have been given in respect of future property. Is it proposed to put these spouses who have relied on these agreements, and who have acquired further properties which may in some cases house children and partner of a second relationship, in a position that on applying for divorce the other spouse can seek orders in respect of this property?;
- the Bill adopts the wording of the existing 1989 provision and therefore allows a divorced person to apply for maintenance at any time after divorce.

The Bill provides that a divorced spouse may still apply for provision from the other's estate. This appears to be the case even where, as commonly happens, succession rights have already been extinguished under the Judicial Separation and Family Law Reform Act 1989.

The notion of community property or marital property is not addressed in the Bill. It would appear that property acquired after separation and even divorce can be the subject matter of division later on.

There is no proposal to limit judicial discretion in any way, even though problems about the amount of discretion given to the courts have arisen in other countries. As we will see, there are international legislative changes to limit judicial discretion in the area of child support.

In the area of division of property, it appears that there should be a starting point of equal distribution, but the court should, in special circumstances, have the ability to award either partner more or less.

The Scottish legislation set out in the Family Law (Scotland)

Act 1985 contains three guiding principles in relation to property division: (Sutherland: 1986-1987)

- the net value of the matrimonial property should be shared fairly, provided that there is a presumption that fair distribution is equal division. Property inherited or received by gift cannot be the subject matter of division, and neither can property acquired before the marriage (except for the family home);
- There is room for the compensatory theory in the provisions that allow the court take into account the economic disadvantages sustained by one of the parties. The court shall have regard to the extent to which economic advantages or disadvantages sustained by either party have been balanced by the economic advantages or disadvantages sustained by the other, and any resulting imbalance has been or will be corrected by a sharing of the matrimonial property or otherwise.
- The economic burden of child-rearing should be shared equally. The court can take into account loss of earning capacity when making any orders.

In Scotland life policies or occupational pensions form part of matrimonial property. This is an attempt to tackle the thorny subject of loss of benefit of a pension. Effectively, actuarial evidence is given as to the value of the pension, and this is included in the value of the assets available for division. This allows for a satisfactory trade-off of the house and the pension. Other legislative solutions have provided for apportionment of the pension right between a divorced spouse and any subsequent spouse. Where there are no assets available for distribution, this would appear to be the most satisfactory solution. (It is included in the reforms to the 1989 Act mentioned above.)

The attraction of the Scottish legislation is that it makes clear the intention and aim of the court orders – self-sufficiency, compensation and a clean break – but at the same time it allows the court enough discretion to depart from these guidelines.

It is worth noting that the previous legislation had been criticised for three weaknesses: the aim of the orders was not stated clearly; the factors relevant to reaching a decision were not seen to be consistent; and the orders which could be made by the court were too limited. Only the final criticism does not apply to the proposed Irish divorce legislation.

CHILDREN AND DIVORCE

Children are affected financially and emotionally by divorce. In one in four cases in Wallerstein's (1980) study there was a sharp difference between the economic status of the children and their father. There is a universal problem with child-support awards and compliance with the orders. Weitzman's survey in California demonstrated that non-compliance with child-support awards was common.

Reforms in the USA, Australia and, most recently, Britain, have removed the issue of child support from the court. This reform came about as a result of evidence that judicial maintenance orders were low, because the courts saw the availability of social security as a factor in reducing awards of maintenance.

The English Child Benefit Act of 1991 provides for the establishment of the Child Support Agency (CSA), which assesses child-support liability according to a formula and enforces it, removing the function of assessing child-support awards from the power of the courts. This implies that the most appropriate way of assessing maintenance is by non-discretionary and non-judicial means.

An alternative model for the assessment of child support is that provided for by the Australian and American legislatures, where a fixed percentage of the parent's income is payable (17 or 18 per cent for one child, with appropriate increases for any additional children).

With the introduction of the 'liable relatives' social-welfare provision there has been some move in Ireland towards the English position. As has been demonstrated in England, however, there are potentially enormous difficulties with this type of legislation. The British arrangements are particularly problematic in cases when there was a clean-break settlement between the spouses and the CSA then seeks a contribution towards support. It is imperative that, should divorce be introduced in Ireland, the social-welfare system should be thoroughly reformed.

PARENTING AFTER DIVORCE

The effect of marital breakdown on children is now acknowledged to be major. Judith Wallerstein's 1980 study of the effects of marital breakdown in California over a period of fifteen years showed that separation or divorce had a profound effect on the children. A nationwide survey in the USA found that 40 per cent of fathers without custody do not visit their children, even though it is now acknowledged that the father–child relationship is crucial and ongoing contact essential to the development of the child. (Furstenberg, 1990)

Commentators emphasise that divorce itself is not the problem. It is better that children live with one parent than with two if those two have an unhappy or destructive relationship. Further, the effects of the divorce can be said to be the same as those of any permanent and sometimes bitter separation of parents. Therefore, families and children in Ireland can be said to suffer the same consequences in cases of separation as children in California suffer after divorce.

The importance of the research and the lesson to be learned from this and other studies is that divorce should be child-centred. Most countries allowing divorce have attempted to acknowledge this fact in their laws.

The legislation governing England and Wales identifies the welfare of the children as being the primary factor to be considered in divorce. The Scottish legislation lists a number of factors to be considered in looking at the economic burden of child-rearing.

In the United States the solution of joint custody was decided upon. This generally means shared physical custody. A number of states (at least 33) have made provision for joint custody, and in some, this is the preferred option. However, ongoing studies of voluntary joint custody do not seem to show that it reduces the effects of divorce or separation. It is, however, useful in encouraging fathers to parent their children and to maintain contact with them. It also assists in allowing women return to the marketplace.

Voluntary joint-custody arrangements were no worse and in some cases better than sole custody. It would appear from initial results of studies, however, that the affect of imposed or court-ordered joint-custody arrangements where one parent strongly opposes them is very detrimental to the children. Wallerstein and Blakeslee (1989) found that in court-ordered joint-custody arrangements children fare even worse than children reared in traditional sole-custody homes.

In England the solution was to remove the concept of custody from the legislation. The Children Act 1989 replaced custody by parental responsibility, defined as being 'all rights, duties, powers, responsibilities and authority which by law a parent has in relation to the child and his property'. This concept is similar to the concept of guardianship in Irish law. Residence orders replace care and control; a residence order gives one parent the right to have a child live with him or her. The order may specify the period during which a child is to live in the different households concerned. As the law is so recent, there are no studies on the long-term effect of these orders.

What is clear is that the affects of any divorce on the welfare of the children will have to be investigated before the courts make an order. Counselling and intervention before the divorce has been recommended. The purpose of this intervention would not be to try to save the marriage, but to enable the spouses to separate in a way that has the least detrimental effect on the children. Both spouses must always separate in their minds the dispute and breakdown in their relationship, and the fact that their children need both parents after separation.

The introduction of divorce would allow a unique opportunity to investigate and provide legislative guidelines in this country. This opportunity is not, however, addressed by the White Paper, and the possibility of statutorily defining joint custody and enabling the court make such orders on consent has not yet been considered. The legislature should also examine the possibility of removing the concept of custody from the legislation.

A BASIS FOR IRISH LEGISLATION

The White Paper fails to identify any aim or rationale of the financial orders available after divorce. All the proposed legislation does is to allow divorced spouses to remarry; the thorny issue of the economic relationship of the divorcing spouses is not addressed.

It is not proposed to give willing spouses the option of agreeing that their economic relationship should end. Do we wish the economic relationship between divorced spouses to continue for life even where they themselves do not? We must avail of the up and coming debate to look at and fully understand the role of women in society and their economic status. The conclusions we can draw from the experience of divorce in other jurisdictions seem to be that:

- listing a number of factors to be considered by the court in deciding financial relief has been proved to be unsatisfactory;
- self-sufficiency should be an aim but provision should be made for women to make the transition from dependency to self-sufficiency;
- a clean break is desirable if there are sufficient assets to do so and if the spouses consent;
- all assets acquired before and during the marriage should be available for division (with some procedure for registering separate property);
- a presumption of equal division is a good starting point but there must be room for special considerations – for example, the provision of purchase funds, compensation for loss of economic advantage, financial hardship, sharing the economic burden of child-rearing;
- older wives must be protected, for example by a presumption that there will be life-long maintenance;
- proper financial provision must be made for children – with a move from the aim of merely meeting a 'need' to one of equalising the living standards in both post-divorce homes;
- pensions should form part of marital property and be subject to division;
- where there are not enough assets for division, consideration should be given to compensatory maintenance, in particular where one party has increased earning potential or obtained professional qualifications with the help of the other spouse.

Irish law provides for joint guardianship even after separation. Shared physical custody should be available only where the spouses agree, and where it is a viable and practical solution. However, emphasis on the involvement of the non-custodial parent on matters such as education, religion and health must be stressed in any divorce legislation. Mediation as a method of resolving disputes about the welfare of children should also be the preferred option.

Finally, as stated above, a complete re-assessment of the social-welfare system will be necessary in the event that divorce becomes available.

This has been an initial and perhaps superficial examination of the issues which may arise in post-divorce Ireland. The challenge now facing us is that of looking at and learning from the experience in other countries so that we can put in place the most effective divorce legislation – legislation which properly protects and secures the rights of all members of the family when marriage breaks down.

REFERENCES

Baliey and Bala, 'Canada: Abortion, Divorce and Poverty and Recognition of Non Traditional Families', *Journal of Family Law* 1991-1992. Vol. 30, 279, 1992.

Ekelaar and Maclean, *Maintenance after Divorce*, Oxford: Oxford Socio-legal Studies, 1986.

Law Commission, *The Financial Consequences of Divorce: The Basic Policy*. No.103, 1980.

Law Commission, *A Discussion Paper on the Grounds for Divorce Law*. No.170, 1988.

Payne, Julien, 'Co-Parenting Revisited'. In Folberg, Jay (Ed.): *Joint Custody and Shared Parenting*, United States Bureau of National Affairs, 1984.

Sutherland, Elaine, 'Scotland, Family Finances and Propery Reformed.' 28 *Journal of Family Law* 1986-1987, 211, 1987.

Wallerstein, J S and Kelly J B, *Surviving the Breakup: How Children and Parents Cope with Divorce*. London: Grant McIntyre, 1980.

Wallerstein, Judith and Blakeslee, S, *Second Chance: Men, women and children, a decade after divorce*. Uxbridge: Bantam Press, 1989.

Ward, Peter, *The Financial Consequences of Marital Breakdown*. Cork: Cork University Press, 1993.

Weitzman, L J, 'Equity and Equality in Divorce Settlements.' In Ekelaar and Butterworth, *Resolution of Family Conflict, A Comparative Legal Perspective*, Toronto: Butterworth, 1984.

Weitzman, L J, *The Divorce Revolution*, New York: The Free Press, 1985.

Social Welfare and Taxation

Mags O'Brien and others

What follows is a brief definition of the social-welfare system as it stands in relation to marital breakdown and foreign divorce. There is also a section on the special tax allowance available to lone parents who are employed. The main items of concern regarding social welfare and taxation are covered; however, as the rules are so complex, individuals with problem cases should look for further details from community advice centres or the local Unemployed Centre.

There are many complaints from separated people about the unfairness of the system and the indignity of means tests. Intrusion into an individual's private life is unwelcome at any time, and it is doubly upsetting for those whose marriages have recently broken down and who are trying to cope with changed circumstances and emotional upheaval. Strict application of rules in certain areas, especially that of supplementary payments, has frequently placed families at risk.

Since the EU forced equal payment in the social-welfare system (a step that should have helped women), the Department of Social Welfare has moved increasingly toward household or family payments in preference to individual payments. Unless the emphasis is shifted to individuals claiming in their own right, unfairness in the system will persist. One hopeful note is that, especially with the new eight-hour ruling for payment of PRSI, more women entering or returning to, the workforce will qualify for benefits in their own right, rather than as dependants.

For those inexperienced in social-welfare and taxation payments, or wanting to clarify the types of problems that arise within the system, the following examples are useful:

A wife is forced to flee the family home and leave her children behind because her husband persistently battered her. She qualifies for assistance only for herself, because her children are not living with her. She is unable to obtain enough assistance to rent a house, and therefore her husband is granted custody of the children because the judge says she cannot provide them with a home. When she finally manages to rent a house, the Community Welfare officer refuses to give her the money for a deposit, but offers her an allowance towards the rent. Obviously she cannot get the house without the deposit.

After many years of separation from her husband, a working woman with children meets an unemployed man with whom she forms a relationship. He moves in with her and they quickly find that:

- her income is taken into account when his means are assessed for social-welfare purposes;
- she loses her single parent tax-free allowance. This means a further annual loss of between £600 and £1,100, depending on her tax rate;
- although they are being treated as a family unit by social welfare and she has lost her single parent tax allowance, she is refused a married person's allowance and tax bands.

These are but two examples of the *Alice through the Looking Glass* social-welfare code.

The following article uses the male as the usual claimant of social welfare in a family, unless stated otherwise, because, under existing rules the Department normally pays money to a husband, and his wife and children are classed as dependants. The former Minister of State at the Department of Social Welfare, Joan Burton TD, who was charged with task of removing anomalies from the tax and social-welfare system, committed herself to dealing with the problem of women as dependants when she stated at an International Women's Conference held in Cork in May, 1993:

The bulk of the Commission on the Status of Women's recommendations dealing with the Social Welfare Code, and with which I am directly concerned, relate to reforming the system, so that women working in the home can receive payments in their own right rather than as dependants of their husbands; so that women in the home can obtain old-age pensions in their own right; so that young lone parents can gain access to training and employment without jeopardising their social-welfare payments; and so that women who are the carers of children and the elderly may be better helped and that the caring role may not be regarded as the exclusive role of women.

The problem that will be encountered by the government in trying to implement such a programme is that treating people as individuals will mean extra costs for the Department of Social Welfare and will therefore be strongly resisted. The present Minister for Social Welfare, Proinsias de Rossa, is presently drafting a Bill to ensure that anyone in receipt of a payment due to marital breakdown will receive exactly the same if divorced.

DETAILS OF SOCIAL-WELFARE/TAXATION RULES

It is difficult to give any general rules about the treatment of non-marital families in the social welfare system. However, it is possible to say that a married couple living together with children, and an unmarried couple living together are treated in broadly the same way, although there are some differences.

The legal situation is that the income of the spouse or cohabitee is taken into account when entitlement to a means-tested payment is being assessed. The total payment to the couple may be restricted if one of them is receiving a means-tested payment. In practice, it is likely that these provisions are always applied to married couples but may, or may not, be applied to unmarried couples.

In general, a married couple living together get less than a married couple living separately. This is because of the restriction in payments to couples where one of them is getting a means-tested payment.

PAYMENTS TO PEOPLE IN BROKEN MARRIAGES

Separate Payments

Usually when a husband receives a social-welfare benefit he also gets an adult dependant allowance for his wife, if she is a dependant, and allowances for any dependent children. If he is not giving money to his wife, she may apply for separate payments. She would then get half of the combined personal adult dependant rate and the child dependant rates. Because of the introduction of the Lone Parent Allowance, this is not so important as it once was, as it is relevant only when the couple are still living in the same household.

Deserted Wives Benefit (DWB)

This is payable on the basis of PRSI contributions, and is paid to a wife who has been deserted. It is restricted to people who earn less than £12,000. It seems likely that the payment will be abolished over the next few years. If you are getting maintenance of more than the appropriate rate of DWB for your family circumstances, you may not qualify for DWB. The provisions relating to liable relatives, set out below, apply to this benefit. As DWB is an insurance-based payment, income from other sources will not affect your entitlement.

How is 'Desertion' Defined?

You may be a deserted wife if your husband left you of his own volition and if you are not subsequently being maintained by him. (The definition of 'maintained' here is exactly the same as in the definition of separated spouse, as defined below). Deserted wives are required to continue to make efforts to get maintenance from their husbands. The special provisions that apply to widows, deserted wives and prisoners' wives do not apply to men in the same situation. Men are required to have dependent children in order to qualify for a Lone Parent Allowance (LPA). The reason for this is that women have historically been considered as dependants under the social welfare codes, many of these regulations having come from a time when married women were discouraged from working.

Deserted wives who have dependent children should apply for the LPA, as they need only to prove separation of three months instead of proving desertion, which is considerably more difficult. Those who would not qualify for the LPA, that is, those over 40 who do not have dependent children, will have to go for the deserted wife's allowance.

Dependent Child

For the purposes of these payments, a dependent child is a child under 18, or between 18 and 21, in full-time education. They must normally live with the lone parent. This means that, as well as having the child live with you, you must have the main care and charge of the child. The regulations do not specify that a child of separately living parents cannot be regarded as a dependant of both, but it is unlikely that two dependent child allowances will be paid. There is no provision for splitting the allowance between the two parents. The tax allowance for lone parents can be granted to each parent if they have custody of the children for part of the time.

Lone Parent Allowance (LPA)

The Lone Parent Allowance may be paid to a widow, a widower, a separated spouse, an unmarried person or a person whose spouse is in prison for at least six months, provided they have at least one dependent child. Normally the child must be living with the person in receipt of payment. This payment is means tested.

Separated spouses: for the purposes of the Lone Parent Allowance you are regarded as separated if you meet two conditions:

- you are not being maintained by your spouse, or, if you are receiving maintenance, it is less than the maximum Lone Parent Allowance you would receive for your family size;
- you and your spouse have lived apart for at least three months continuously, immediately before you claim the allowance. If you are separated you are obliged to make, and continue to make, appropriate efforts to get maintenance.

If each separated spouse has a dependent child living with her or him, they should each qualify for the Lone Parent Allowance as a separated spouse.

Lone parents without dependent children: while widows may qualify for a non-contributory pension whether or not they have children, deserted wives or prisoners' wives who are under 40 years of age must have a dependent child in order to qualify. Those over 40 may qualify for deserted/prisoner's wives allowance without having a child.

The Means Test

The LPA means test takes into account income from all sources. You may earn £6 per week in respect of each dependent child before your earnings are taken into account. After that, if you have means of up to £6 per week you may still qualify for the full amount of the payment, provided you have no other income.

So if you have three children you could earn £18 per week and still qualify for the full payment.

There is also an administrative practice of allowing a deduction in the means test for payments to child-minders.

The yearly value of any capital you have is assessed as follows: the first £200 is not included and £100 in respect of each dependent child is also excluded. After that, you are assumed to have an income of five per cent of the remainder. In other words, it is assumed that you are getting a return of five per cent on your capital.

The effect of maintenance payments on the social welfare payment is described below.

LIABILITY TO MAINTAIN FAMILY

The Social Welfare Act 1989 included provisions dealing with the liability of spouses to support each other and their children. These provisions were brought into force in November 1990 and have been modified by the Social Welfare Act of 1992.

These provisions mean that for the purposes of the Lone Parents Allowance, Deserted Wives Wllowance, Deserted Wives Benefit and Supplementary Welfare Allowance, there is an obligation on each spouse to maintain the other and to maintain their children. In the case of an unmarried parent, the liability is in respect of the children only; there is no liability on the part of one parent to maintain the other. The children are liable to be maintained up to the age of 18 and, for Lone Parent/Deserted Wives payments, up to 21 years of age if in full-time education. This is a different liability from that which arises under the maintenance legislation described above (ie where the other spouse has to take action to get payments). What the social welfare provisions mean is that if you fail to maintain your dependent spouse or child, the Department of Social Welfare and the Health Boards (in the case of the SWA) have the power to pursue you and force you to do so. As is mentioned already, spouses who are seeking Lone Parents payments are expected to have made and to continue to make efforts to get maintenance from their spouses.

If you are granted a Lone Parent or Deserted Wife's payment, the Department of Social Welfare may try to find your spouse and decide how much he/she should contribute. (The Health Boards have the same powers in respect of

Supplementary Welfare Allowance payments to separated spouses, but there is no information available as to whether they use them or not.) The Department may go to court to get an order directing the spouse to contribute. The Department initially decides how much the spouse should contribute. There are no statutory rules about how this is to be decided, but a means test is applied as follows:

Take your gross income from all sources; deduct income tax and PRSI contributions. You then get a personal allowance which is the same as the personal weekly rate of benefit paid to your spouse; if dependant children are living with you, you get an allowance for each of them of the amount of the child dependent rate of LPA. You may then get an allowance of up to £75 per week (£300 a month) if you have to pay a mortgage or rent for your accommodation; you will be allowed only half of these costs if you have an adult partner living with you who earns more than £55 per week and who is not getting a social-welfare payment. You may also get an allowance in respect of the family home if you are paying the mortgage and the spouse still lives there. After all these allowances, the rest of your income is available for contribution to the Department. The maximum contribution you will have to make is the net payment by the Department to your spouse.

Having decided how much you should contribute, the Department will ask you for the contribution. If you fail to pay, they may then apply to the District Court for an order directing you to pay. If you still fail to pay, the Department may pursue normal civil debt proceedings. Since the passing of the 1992 Social Welfare Act the Department is more likely to ask the District Court to make an Attachment of Earnings Order if the liable relative is in employment. This will operate in broadly the same way as it does for maintenance orders. According to the Department of Social Weflare, the number of cases examined since 1990 is 10,120. These are broken down as follows:

	%
Employed/Self-Employed:	22
On Social Welfare:	47
No Trace:	31

While opponents of divorce argue that it will be a cost to the taxpayer, it should be noted that this cost already exists with separation. What is also evident from the above figures is that 47 per cent of those pursued were on social welfare payments. This implies that their wives/families have merely shifted from one payment to another, rather than being a further cost on the state.

EFFECT OF MAINTENANCE PAYMENTS ON THE LONE PARENT ALLOWANCE

The first thing to remember is that you will not qualify for a Lone Parent payment at all if you are receiving maintenance which is more than the appropriate rate of lone parent allowance for your family.

When the liable relatives provisions were brought into effect in November 1990, people who were already receiving maintenance payments under maintenance orders were able to keep these payments and also receive the LPA or similar payment. People who subsequently got maintenance orders were able to transfer payments under those orders to the Department of Social Welfare. The liability to transfer such payments has now been extended to all recipients of LPA and similar payments. The collection of maintenance by the Department rather than through the court ensures that the dependent receives a payment even if their spouse defaults on payment. While this method undoubtedly is of assistance in ensuring a regular payment, it seems the reasoning behind it had as much to do with reducing social welfare payouts as concern for the welfare of dependants.

The Department has begun to circulate letters to those recieving the above payments and, while they are stressing that the signing-over of maintenance agreements to the Department is voluntary, they state that in the event of non-compliance they may go to court. Many women who were in receipt of a maintenance order over and above the payment that they received from the state have outgoings to match their incomes. While fairness in a system must be maintained, dramatically to reduce the income of a family is traumatic, to say the least, and the Department should have looked at either giving notice of intention to so reduce income, or phasing in the recovery of such money. The reality is that the first most women heard about this was a letter from the Department, with no detailed explanation of the Act itself.

Voluntary Maintenance
Previously it was the case that if a woman were receiving voluntary maintenance, that is maintenance paid without a court order, that maintenance was assessed in the means test for LPA. The amount of maintenance was divided between the dependent members of the family, and the amount attributable to the wife was assessed as her means. Now, the practice is to ignore voluntary maintenance and assess the husband as a liable relative. So, presumably, in these cases the husband will stop paying maintenance to the wife and pay it to the Department instead.

Maintenance Order
The situation is the same under both the 1976 Act and the Judicial Separation Act. The situation previously was that the part of the order that related to the wife's maintenance was taken into account as means. Now, however, the husband will be assessed as a liable relative. If the amount of the assessment is more than he is currently paying in maintenance, he will pay the extra to the Department and the Department may ask the wife to transfer the maintenance order to them. The net effect of this is that the wife would receive only the amount of the LPA. Any maintenance would eventually go to the Department. Theoretically, at least, the wife is still obliged to go to court for maintenance, even though the Department may subsequently go to court to recover contributions from the liable relative (see above).

Annulled Marriages
An annulled marriage – that is, a marriage that has been annulled in state proceedings – is not a marriage any more, so there is no right to claim maintenance from a former spouse in respect of yourself. There is, of course, a right to claim in respect of children.

You may be entitled to a lone parent allowance in the same way as other lone parents. If your former spouse dies, you would not be entitled to a widow's pension.

Foreign divorce

If there is a valid foreign divorce, again, there is no marriage and you have no right to seek maintenance in respect of yourself. Of course, it is possible that there may be provision under the terms of the foreign divorce that maintenance be paid.

You may be entitled to a lone parent allowance if you meet the conditions that normally apply. If your spouse dies, you are not entitled to a widow's pension.

GETTING ANY OF THESE PAYMENTS

There are 22,083 people receiving a Deserted Wife's payment or lone parent allowance for separated spouses (1993 figures). All of these payments, and all administration relating to establishing liability, is done from the Department of Social Welfare, Pension Offices, Sligo.

PRSI

A wife who is receiving maintenance payments which are taxable in her hands may also be liable for PRSI contributions (Class S). This has arisen since PRSI for the self-employed was introduced. The rules about paying self-employed PRSI are quite complex but, in general, if a wife has income of over £2,500 a year she may be liable. She may also be liable for the health and employment levies. This applies even if the husband has already paid levies on that income. Liability for PRSI may arise if the maintenance itself is greater than £2,500 a year. There may be no tax liability but, nevertheless, the payment for PRSI and levies is due on 1 October each year whether you are asked for it or not.

TAXATION

The taxation rules for marriage breakdown and non-marital families are also rather complex.

Separation

Separated people are still legally married and may opt to be taxed as a married couple (if they are both living in the state), and to choose from one of the options for married couples. The information here relates to separation agreements made after 7 June 1983. People who separated before that date may opt (jointly and in writing, or by negotiating a new separation agreement) for the more favourable post-1983 arrangements. In order to be treated as separated for tax purposes you must either:

- have a court order of separation; or
- have a deed of separation; or
- be actually separated in such circumstances that the separation is likely to be permanent.

If you choose to be taxed as a married couple, any maintenance payments are ignored in the tax calculations. The husband pays tax on all his income and pays maintenance from his taxed income. The wife does not pay any tax on the maintenance she receives.

If you do not opt to be treated as a married couple, the arrangements are as follows.

- Each of you is taxed as a single person, gets the single person's allowances and the single person's tax bands.
- The husband pays maintenance to the wife without deducting tax from it.
- The husband is not taxed on the amount he pays in maintenance to his wife; he is liable for tax on the rest of his income. This means he is liable for tax on the amount of maintenance he pays for his children. The wife is liable to tax on the maintenance she receives together with any income she may have.
- One or both may be entitled to the single parent tax allowance.

Which Option?

A separated couple need to look very carefully at how they arrange their tax. If they decide to be taxed as a married couple, then neither may claim the single parent allowance but they can get the married rate of mortgage allowance and other expenditure reliefs. These expenditure reliefs are available only to the person incurring the expenditure, so, if the husband is paying the mortgage, he can get the single person's mortgage allowance only if the couple are not being taxed as a married couple. The wife cannot get any mortgage allowance because she is not paying it.

Taxation

At present a single person is entitled to £2,350 tax-free allowance and mortgage relief to a maximum of £2,500 (depending on the total amount of interest payable). A married couple are entitled to double this. If both are earning they may decide to split the allowances. If one partner ceases work then the other may claim the double tax allowances. Depending on the amount of earnings they may pay tax at the higher rate, but can also claim the double Table B allowance. (See illustration following.)

When a couple separate, in the first year the 'assessable spouse' keeps the married allowance for the year but is is assessed on the double income up to the date of separation. The other spouse (usually the woman) can claim a single allowance for the full year.

If there are children, the single parent allowance is payable to the parent with whom the child(ren) lives, however if the child(ren) spend, for example, a week in turn with each parent, then both parents are entitled to the single allowance.

Problems arise if, for instance, a single man (Joe) moves in with a separated woman (Ann) into a house that she has a mortgage on. Only she can claim the interest relief, even if he is contributing to the mortgage. Also, if Ann has a child, she is no longer entitled to the single parent tax allowance because she is cohabiting. Joe would have to have his name put on the deeds in order to claim tax and this would involve stamp duty being paid, as well as solicitors' fees.

If Ann were single, however, and she and Joe subsequently married, they would be able to claim the double tax allowance.

If Joe and Ann decide to buy a house between them, then they are both entitled to the mortgage relief and to their own personal allowances, but if Ann gave up work Joe would not be able to claim her allowance, which he could if they were married.

A married man whose wife ceases work can claim, over and above his allowances, her personal allowance of £2,350, up to £2,500 extra in interest relief and is allowed to earn a further £8,200 before being taxed at a higher tax rate. The potential difference is around £2,750, depending on total earnings and amount of mortgage relief.

Unmarried Couples (including second relationships)

Unmarried couples who live together are taxed as single people. They cannot opt for any other tax treatment and, therefore, there is no tax relief available even if one partner is actually dependent on the other. (See explanation above.) If there are children, neither parent can get the single parent family allowance because of cohabitation provisions. One of the consequences of this legislation is that there is almost never a financial incentive to work for those unmarried couples who are receiving social-welfare benefits.

Single Parent Tax Allowance

This allowance may be claimed by the head of a one-parent family if that parent is unable to get a married allowance. It is available to unmarried, widowed, separated, deserted or divorced parents who have a qualifying child residing with them for all or part of the year. The amount of the allowance is £1,600 for a widowed parent and £2,100 for others. It is available to the parent with whom the child lives – if the child spends part of the time with each parent then each may qualify for the allowance. A single parent who is cohabiting is not entitled to the allowance. The child must be aged 16, or if over that age, must be either in full-time education or permanently incapacitated (if aged over 21 s/he must have become incapacitated before that age).

If the child has income in their own right, the allowance may be reduced by the amount that income exceeds £720. Income from scholarships, grants et cetera is not taken into account. Single parents who covenant to their children may lose some of the one-parent family allowance if they covenant more than £720 per year. As and from 1996, however, these will be abolished.

SOCIAL WELFARE AND DIVORCE

During the build-up to the 1986 divorce referendum, much was made of the fact that deserted wives would lose their benefits if their husbands divorced them. The introduction of the lone parent allowance has changed this perception somewhat, although there are still differences with regard to the Deserted Wives' Benefit. There have been strong indications that the DWB will be abolished in the near future, meaning effectively that separated and divorced women will be treated in exactly the same manner by the Department of Social Welfare. Therefore, divorce will not affect payments. Obviously there is a necessity for a move toward payments to individuals in their own right, regardless of marital status.

The only category where divorce would affect payments is that of widows/widowers. At present if a man divorces his wife in another jurisdiction and subsequently dies, she is not entitled to a widow's pension. This provision would also apply to Irish divorces if they were made legal. Obviously any settlement should have included maintenance and pension rights, if a pension was in existence (see chapter on Occupational Pension). If this was not the case and there are dependent children, the ex-wife would qualify for a lone parent allowance. (A Widower's Pension has now been introduced.)

CONCLUSION

While there are no easy solutions to resolving the anomalies in the social-welfare system affecting separated persons, there is a real need to tackle them regardless of the introduction of divorce. Consider the 1991 census figures on marital breakdown in Ireland. While there were 55,143 separated people, the breakdown showed that 33,793 women but only 21,350 men classified themselves as separated. Presumably a large portion of the missing 12,443 men are domiciled abroad, and there is a likelihood of them obtaining a legal foreign divorce in the future. As already illustrated, these divorces affect the tax and pension standing of the ex-wives (and of course any deserted husbands) remaining in Ireland. These problems must be addressed, regardless of the outcome of any future divorce referendum.

Divorce, Separation and Occupational Pensions

Rosheen Callender

In the context of separation and divorce, a number of important and complex issues arise where one or both partners are members of an occupational pension scheme. One such issue is whether pension rights should always be seen as part of the 'marital property' and divided up, somehow, between the parties on divorce. If the answer to this is 'yes', or 'usually', then further questions arise: like 'how exactly?', 'when?' and 'who decides?'. These lead, in turn, to a host of subsidiary questions and complications.

Only one thing is for sure: this is not a matter which lends itself to easy answers or cut-and-dried solutions which will fit every case in a way that is absolutely fair to all concerned. There is simply too much variety – within marriages and within occupational-pension arrangements – for this to be so. It's also important to bear in mind that people can bring very different 'assets' and 'property' to a marriage, some with a clear monetary value and some without; and they can make very different contributions, both monetary and non-monetary, during a marriage. Moreover, a non-monetary contribution, such as the unpaid labour of one partner (usually the woman) can add enormously to the monetary remuneration, both present and future, of the other partner. Taking account of this, and trying to quantify it, in a way which is fair to all concerned, is no easy task. It is particularly difficult if it is seen as important to avoid apportioning 'blame' and 'guilt' to one or other partner; and to share out assets according to need as well as 'who contributed what'.

Take as an example the following case:

Anna and Brian married when she was 22 and he was 25. She was a clerical worker who had left school at 18 and had worked in a small office since then; he was an unskilled worker, employed sporadically in the building industry. In the early years of the marriage, she supported him while he studied for a professional qualification. He later found 'permanent and pensionable' employment. After a while, they started a family. At

105

30, after 12 years of full-time work, she left what by then had become a low-paid, dead-end job – with no pension rights – to look after the home and family, release Brian from the domestic duties he'd shared when they both worked, and leave him freer to pursue his more rewarding career.

Then, at 45, with two teenage children, Anna finds that the 23-year-old marriage is over. The decision to separate is mutual, and initially there is no acrimony over division of the marital assets. Brian will support the children to the end of third-level education, if they go to college, which he wants them to do. Anna will keep the family home and he'll also support her, for a while, till she updates her secretarial skills (a short computer course) and gets back to work. However, she then begins to feel that he should either support her until she gets a degree and a better job – which will take longer – or should pay her a much higher proportion than he is offering of the income, both present and future (including pension rights) that she helped him to secure...After all, divorce would mean the loss of a substantial death-in-service benefit if Brian should die prematurely, and a substantial widow's benefit if he dies after retirement.

No simple, fixed formula will do justice to this situation and all others. Anna has clearly contributed to the build-up of Brian's present and future income through both paid and unpaid labour on her part. Yet she has no independent income or pension rights of her own to show for it. Brian's pension isn't worth much yet, but it will be by the time he retires. By then, she may or may not have some pension rights herself. If she has, they are unlikely to be very significant (if indeed she manages to get into a pension scheme at all when pushing 50). If, perchance, she remarries, it's by no means certain that her new husband will provide adequate pension cover for her. He too may have had a previous marriage and prior commitments in relation to his assets. In this situation allocating part of Brian's pension rights to Anna, in proportion to the length of the marriage, might seem unfair because during most of that time he wasn't in a pension scheme; but allocating pension rights in proportion to the time of membership of the scheme before the break-up could seem equally unfair. And who knows what will happen either of them after the age of 50?

In the end, the parties themselves, with their solicitors and with or without the courts, will have to agree on what's fair, in all the circumstances of each individual case. Yet leaving everything, ultimately, to the courts is not necessarily the best solution: there must also be general guidelines and principles to be followed. We need to find the best possible balance between laying down minimum entitlements, but also respecting individual arrangements, where these are mutually agreed. Even then, the 'minimum rights, maximum flexibility' approach runs the risk of becoming a formula for settlements which will in some cases seem too low.

There is a lot to be learnt from the experience of other countries in this regard; and one of the very few advantages in Ireland delaying so long over the introduction of divorce is that we can perhaps benefit from this. In England and Wales, for example, there are some very general guidelines, but no set procedures, for the treatment of pension rights on divorce: the courts decide each case on its merits and have had some difficulty interpreting such vague directions as the need to take account of the parties' income and earning capacity 'in the foreseeable future'. In Scotland, on the other hand, pension benefits are specifically included in the definition of matrimonial property to be divided on divorce – though the courts are not told how exactly they should value them. But in neither jurisdiction do the courts have the power to enforce divorce settlements on pension schemes; and this is in contrast to the USA law, which does give the courts this right. However, the USA courts cannot oblige pension trustees to pay out benefits that are not already provided for in the particular scheme, or benefits that will increase the total cost of the member's entitlements.

In the countries which do attempt to lay down a method of valuing the pension benefits that should be divided on divorce, approaches vary. In South Africa, the law says specifically that they should be based on the amount the member would have received if s/he had resigned on the date of divorce. (This wouldn't have suited Anna, in our example above, since Brian had only a few years' membership of the scheme when the 23-year-old marriage ended.) In New Zealand, on the other hand, the courts have said that pension values should reflect the member's entitlements at retirement, rather than at the time of divorce (and this might not suit Brian, particularly if, by then, he has had a new partner for many years. However, it would give Anna some benefit from his future salary increases – increases that she had helped him to secure, through her efforts prior to their divorce.)

There are certain difficulties about trying to estimate the future value of a pension benefit; and yet, looking at the case of Anna and Brian, there may well be good reasons, in equity, for trying to do so. The difficulties obviously increase the further the couple's ages are from the normal retirement age set down in the pension scheme concerned. Forecasting investment returns and real rates of growth is a tricky business; yet these are major determinants of the future value of a pension. It's also difficult – and rather delicate – to make assumptions and forecasts about how long people are likely to live, how their health will hold up, whether they will stay in the same job until they retire, whether the job itself will stay in existence, and whether the pension scheme will stay the same. The assumptions are likely to vary, from actuary to actuary, and may not in all cases hold true. Legislation, or strict guidelines, could eliminate a lot of the variation but would not necessarily ensure accuracy or equity.

There is also the awkward issue of whether or not a pension benefit, or part of it, should be paid out in advance of the contingency for which it was originally intended, eg retirement, incapacity or death. (If two people are divorcing, and both are age 45, why should one receive a benefit of some kind immediately, if the other has to wait, eg until 65?) On the other hand, it is generally seen as undesirable to make divorcing couples wait until one of these contingencies occur before payments can be made. Thus in New Zealand, even though the benefits are calculated on the basis of retirement rather than withdrawal values, they also specify that couples should not necessarily have to wait until retirement in order to receive any benefit.

The conclusion would seem to be that no single formula will be appropriate, in every case, for quantifying the value of pension benefits to which one or both partners may become entitled at a future date. However, it is important that certain guiding principles are agreed, and perhaps laid down in a Code of Practice, to help couples who are separating or divorcing to reach equitable settlements, with the help of their legal advisors and in some cases the courts. With such guidelines in place, there is no reason why a fair settlement cannot be reached, in the vast majority of cases, whatever technical, actuarial and mathematical complexities might arise. (This is not to say, of course, that all settlements will be adequate – as opposed to fair – since in some cases, where assets and incomes are already low, their division may cause financial hardship however 'fair' the share-out.) The guiding principles for dividing pension entitlements might include the following.

In most cases, pension rights should be seen as part of the 'marital property', to be shared fairly between the spouses. The exceptions might be where there are no children and the partners each have similar earning capacities and similar pension entitlements in their own right, the marriage has been of short duration and the divorce occurs when both are relatively young. Alternatively, in some cases, the pension might just be seen as a basis for continuing an agreed level of maintenance payment (eg an ex-spouse gets x per cent of the other spouse's earnings while s/he is working and then the same per cent of his/her pension when retirement occurs – leaving the full entitlement to come, initially, to the pensioner rather than apportioning or earmarking some of it to the ex-spouse. Of course, the success of this approach depends entirely on maintenance orders and agreements being strictly enforced or voluntarily honoured.

In a few cases, for example where one partner has substantial pension rights, both partners are approaching retirement age and no re-marriage is envisaged, it may be possible to leave retirement benefits intact and simply allocate a proportion of the pension and death benefit directly to the divorced spouse (something known as 'pension splitting'). In funded, defined benefit pension schemes, the withholding of any part of a retirement benefits package, on grounds of divorce, where there is no other payee – ie no new partner – would constitute a windfall gain for the pension fund concerned. In such cases, the gain will ultimately revert to the employer; this would be unfair and unwarranted, particularly where the ex-spouse has no other source of income.

In other cases, where again both partners are approaching retirement age, but only one partner has pension rights and re-marriage (by the pensionable partner) is envisaged, the retirement benefits (ie both the pension and death benefits) should be allocated roughly in proportion to the length of the marriage –

taking account of other relevant factors such as the incomes and earning capacities of both partners and the value of any non-monetary or 'un-pensioned' contributions which have been made and which have enhanced the value of the other partner's income and pension rights. This may of course be a somewhat subjective calculation but then so are many others that actuaries have to attempt.

Where divorce occurs well before retirement age, but substantial pension rights have nevertheless accrued, or are clearly starting to accrue, the mathematics of apportioning them fairly will be even further complicated by the length of time between divorce and retirement. Clearly, the bigger this gap, the greater the uncertainty about the accuracy of actuarial predictions and calculations, as well as the continued 'pensionability' of the partner with the retirement benefits. Yet in many cases it may be fairer to a first spouse to base the calculations on the value of the pension at retirement, rather than at the time of the divorce.

The issue of continuing life cover is also important where divorce occurs at relatively early ages, especially where there are young, dependent children.

Despite the mathematical and other difficulties, it is important to have clarity on these matters at the time of the divorce. It is essential to avoid situations in which former spouses have a vested – and usually unhealthy – interest in each other's subsequent financial or marital situation. The rights of one ex-spouse must in no way depend on whether or not the other re-marries, or how rich or poor the new partner(s) might be. In this respect, divorce is fundamentally different from separation, where the partners remain married and where a major change in the financial circumstances of one remains a legitimate concern of the other, insofar as it can form valid grounds for alteration of the separation terms.

Once the primary problem of 'fair apportionment' of pension rights has been solved, the secondary issue of what form these rights should take must be settled. This may not always be easy either. In some cases, the entitlements of the ex-spouse, once valued, can be transferred into a personal retirement bond or annuity, in the name of that person. Then he or she should have full 'sight' and control of it and be kept informed, directly, of its progress and what it can reasonably be expected to yield when an eventuality such as death, or reaching a certain age, occurs. In other cases, there may be good reasons to leave the benefit – suitably 'earmarked' – in its existing pension scheme. If so, the ex-spouse should be able to retain the benefit without fear of any future loss or confusion about his or her entitlements. Either way, the ex-spouse should have distinct and separate information rights – which means, specifically, that the Pensions Act 1990 and relevant Regulations should be amended to ensure that this is provided directly and automatically, each year. Finally, unless the value of the benefit is very small, the benefit should not be 'sold' for immediate cash: it should serve to provide an income in retirement (or at death), as is its purpose.

When both divorcing partners have independent incomes and pension rights, it may be possible to leave each more or less intact, especially if they are at similar levels – thus avoiding all the complications of apportioning and valuing present and future retirement benefits. Inequalities can be remedied by other means such as cash settlements and/or division of other assets. However, it must never be assumed that mere membership of similar pension schemes will result in similar benefits, as one partner's 'pensionable pay' and 'pensionable service' might be far more than the other's, resulting in very different benefits. Nor should it be assumed, simply because both partners worked outside the home, that they each made equal contributions within that home – or that the disproportionate domestic contribution of one partner had no beneficial financial implications for the other. So in the end, the 'balancing' and 'weighing-up' in such cases could be every bit as complex as for the one-income couple. And it will be just as important to get it right, since two-income couples are increasing in number and will presumably feature in equal proportions to other couples, in future divorce statistics.

When a fair settlement has been reached, either by agreement or through the courts, there must be appropriate mechanisms (court orders, if necessary) to ensure that the agreement is enforced and that pension fund trustees take the necessary steps to split, earmark or transfer benefits and (if the ex-spouse's benefits are remaining within the scheme) to ensure that he or she receives relevant information, directly, each year.

Finally, as regards apportionment of retirement and death benefits, it is worth noting that although the Status of Children

Act, 1987 has outlawed all discrimination against 'non-marital', as opposed to 'marital', children, not all pension schemes have altered their rules accordingly. Overriding legislation should be introduced to ensure that even in those schemes which have not yet changed their rules, no children can be disadvantaged because of their parents' marital status. This may of course give rise to some administrative difficulties (eg where a man has several extra-marital children with different mothers) but the number of such cases may well decline after the introduction of divorce and the right to re-marry.

The foregoing does not, of course, comprehensively cover all the complex technical points which need to be addressed in detail before divorce legislation is introduced, so that people can be reassured that there is a way of dealing fairly with every situation, no matter how awkward the calculations and the 'balancing' of rights and interests. It does not deal, for example, with the need for many occupational pension schemes, in both the public and private sectors, to change their rules in certain respects (even if there is overriding legislation). It does not deal with the need for certain anomalies to be removed from the tax system: at present, the Capital Acquisitions Tax threshold is only £11,000 for cohabitees, divorced people and spouses whose marriages have been annulled by the state, whereas inheritances between spouses are completely tax-exempt. Nor does it deal with the question of revaluing, or index-linking, a pension benefit which has been allocated to an ex-spouse and has either been transferred out of the original scheme, or has been left in the original scheme, but the member spouse has left the employment before normal retirement age. However, these and other issues must be addressed in due course; and once general guiding principles are agreed, it will be easier to envisage a situation in which the rights and interests of all parties affected by divorce are fully recognised and protected.

POSTSCRIPT

The foregoing was written in mid-1993, prior to the publication of the Family Law Bill, 1994 and the subsequent change of government at the end of 1994. The Family Law Bill, 1994 proposed to give the courts the right to determine how pension entitlements are divided, in cases where a divorcing or separating couple cannot agree. Basically it gave the courts the right to order financial compensation for the loss of pension entitlements, or require a spouse to give over his or her interest in a life policy to the other spouse, or to take out a special life assurance policy in favour of the other spouse and/or any dependent children, or to make a pensions order which will either 'split' or 'earmark' pension rights. The 'pension-splitting' order would reduce the pension rights of the pensionable spouse and give over certain rights to the other spouse, who would thereafter enjoy quite separate and independent entitlements (either in the original scheme or under some other arrangement approved by the court). The 'pension earmarking' order, on the other hand, would involve the ex-spouse retaining an interest in his or her former spouse's pension and death benefits, with the court deciding on the proportions either at the time of the divorce, or later, as it considers appropriate. In either case, the trustees of the pension scheme concerned would have to be informed and their views, if any, would have to be taken into account by the court.

Finally, under the Family Law Bill 1994, it was proposed that in separation cases, the courts could simply order trustees not to let the separation disqualify a spouse from benefiting under a pension scheme (eg in schemes which require the spouses to be living together at the time of retirement or death in order to qualify for payment). These provisions, if enacted by the new government, would provide sufficient flexibility to the courts to make fair settlements in a variety of situations. However, they do not specifically cover a number of the issues raised above, namely:

- whether and to what extent the courts must take account of the value of 'unpaid and unpensioned' work when determining the division of pension rights (NB this may well be most problematic where both spouses have acquired pension rights but where these rights are very unequal);
- the provision of distinct and separate information rights (eg an annual benefit statement) to ex-spouses with 'split' or 'earmarked' pension rights;
- the revaluation of 'split' pension rights where the spouse who is a member of the pension scheme leaves the employment

before retirement age. (Under the Pensions Act, 1990, the revaluation of early leavers' pensions begins in 1996.)
• specific protection for non-marital children.

The 1994 Bill gave the courts a variety of options, in relation to pension rights; and this is to be welcomed. However, where such rights are to be divided, it effectively came down in favour of the idea of dividing them at the time of payment (ie at death or retirement), rather than at the time of separation or divorce. This has the advantage of greater accuracy, and perhaps equity, because it will clearly be easier to determine the real value of the benefits by then. Anything can happen in the meantime, especially if both are relatively young at the time of the break-up.

However, the 'clean break' approach has its merits and attractions too: it avoids the 'continuing connection' and the often unwelcome and unhealthy vested interest of ex-spouses in each other's subsequent financial, employment and marital status. By allowing for pension rights to be either split or earmarked at the time of the divorce *or at any time thereafter*, the Bill would seem to preserve the right of an ex-spouse to indefinitely maintain a vested interest of this kind.

It goes without saying, of course, that in some cases occupational pensions, however fairly divided between divorcing or separating couples, will simply not stretch to provide adequate incomes for both, particularly if each of them subsequently find themselves on low incomes, or with new dependants, or both. In order to avoid situations of post-divorce poverty – or indeed situations where unhappy partners must stay together 'for the sake of the pension' – it is essential for the social welfare system to provide adequate income support to those who require it, and for whom occupational pensions are insufficient or non-existent.

The question of social-welfare pensions is covered elsewhere. Such pensions are currently payable to survivors only if the spouses were legally married at the date of death. There is no requirement that the spouses be living together at the time of death, so separation (legal or otherwise) does not remove entitlement to a survivor's pension – although a foreign divorce does, if it is recognised by the Irish courts. So does a civil annulment, which has the effect of dissolving a legal marriage.

114

The Churches
The legal requirements for marriage in Ireland and the differing attitudes of various churches to divorce and re-marriage

Mags O'Brien

THE LEGAL REQUIREMENTS FOR MARRIAGE IN IRELAND

Because the Roman Catholic Church performs the vast majority of weddings in Ireland, there is little notice taken of the legal requirements for marriage, and few people realise that there is a civil aspect to church marriages until they encounter problems. In France, for instance, there is a separate civil and religious ceremony, and in England most Roman Catholic weddings require the presence of a State Registrar. Although the Constitution does not endow any religion, in practice Roman Catholics have a privileged position in Irish law. (I use the term Roman Catholic for clarity as other denominations also regard themselves as Catholics). If a RC couple wish to marry, the only formalities which apply are the celebration of the marriage by a priest, and parental consent if either of them is under age. The other religions have to have the following in order that the state recognise their ceremony.

Roman Catholic Church mixed marriage: ordinary licence or registrar's certificate.

Presbyterians: published banns or ordinary or special licence.

Church of Ireland: as above; also a registrar's certificate for a church wedding.

Jewish: special licence or a registrar's certificate.

Society of Friends: special licence from the Clerk to the Yearly Meeting or registrar's certificate.

'Other Protestant': special licence, registrar's certificate or registrar's licence.

'Other Christian': registrar's certificate or registrar's licence.

Registry Office: registrar's certificate or registrar's licence.

As the Islamic, Buddhist, Hindu, Sikh and Coptic places of worship in Ireland are not registered with the Registrar's Office, members of these faiths who wish to contract a legal marriage in the state must marry in a Registry Office. Obviously it is then a matter for themselves if they wish to go through a religious ceremony.

The special and ordinary licence are issued by the authorities of the relevant church. A special licence allows a couple to marry at any convenient time and place in Ireland; however, the ordinary licence is more restrictive as the couple must give notice of the marriage and must swear that they have fulfilled residence requirements and that there is no lawful impediment to the marriage.

The Registrar's certificate and licence are issued by a state registrar. The requirements are the same as for an ordinary church licence. One interesting point is that if a marriage is performed in a registry office and one of the parties state that s/he has had a usual place of worship for a month before, a copy of the notice will be hung in the Registrar's Office. If there is no place of worship stated, then the couple are obliged, at their own expense, to publish notice of the marriage for two consecutive weeks in a newspaper.

'Knowing and wilful' non-observance of these complex procedures can make a marriage null and void. So too can:

• marrying in a place other than stated in the notice/ licence/certificate;
• marrying in a place other than where the banns have been read;
• marrying after the notice/licence/certificate has expired;
• marrying without two witnesses.

Non-observance of the formalities relating to residence requirement and parental consent is not, however fatal to the marriage.

It could be argued that these varying requirements may be unconstitutional because they discriminate on the basis of religion, giving the Roman Catholic Church preferential treatment under the law.

Clearly the issuing of specific licences for all churches other than Roman Catholic may serve to emphasise the contractual element for couples. The closeness of the RC Church and the state in this instance causes major confusion when marriages break down and couples seek an annulment.

STATE ANNULMENTS

Between twenty and thirty of these are granted a year, and the criteria, while extremely strict, have been widened somewhat over the last few years. Annulments can be granted only at High Court level or upwards, and a straightforward one costs between £6,000 and £8,000.

The most common reasons for annulment are insanity; lack of consent of one partner; non-consummation of the marriage; homosexuality and lesbianism. One recent case shows how the lack of consent clause has been widened: a woman who was pregnant when she married obtained a decree of nullity on the grounds that she would have lost standing in her profession (teacher) if she had not married.

As a state annulment finds that no marriage existed, it follows therefore that either or both parties may marry in Ireland in the future.

CHURCH ANNULMENTS

The Roman Catholic church grants approximately 200 annulments a year. These have no legal standing and, consequently, neither does any subsequent marriage. The Church has frequently performed marriages of couples with Church annulments but these are actually bigamous. As stated, the Roman Catholic priests are acting as agents of the state when they perform a marriage ceremony. There is a common misconception that, providing the register is not signed, no law has been broken; however, this is not the case. The legal obligation to inform the registrar of a marriage rests with the male marrying; however, the penalty for not informing the registrar is a fine, and the marriage is not null and void. In practice, the priest normally informs the registrar of weddings and therefore the obligation on the man is not normally evident.

ATTITUDES OF VARIOUS RELIGIOUS DENOMINATIONS IN IRELAND TO DIVORCE AND SUBSEQUENT MARRIAGES

In order to ascertain the attitude towards divorce of the various religious denominations in Ireland, the author asked the following questions as general guidelines on the issue. Those churches not listed either had small numbers of members in Ireland, did not answer the survey, or sent literature that did not address the questions asked directly. Those who did respond could not have been more co-operative and courteous.

- Has your faith ever allowed divorce in certain circumstances?
- Does it presently recognise divorce?
- Will you re-marry divorced persons?
- If so, is the ceremony different in any way than your usual wedding ceremony?
- Is there more than one school of thought on the subject among your members?
- Do you feel that the changes in society will necessitate a more tolerant stance amongst your followers on the subject?
- Are you losing members because of your stance on marital breakdown?
- Do you have support groups for families in such circumstances?
- Do you find the present ban on divorce in the Constitution an infringement of your civil liberties?
- Approximately how many followers do you have in Ireland?

The Baha'í Faith. Followers in Ireland: 500 approx
The Baha'ís follow the law of the land in which they live. While they feel that divorce should be a last resort, they would allow it among their followers if it were introduced in Ireland, but would insist on a year's waiting period during which they would expect the couple to make every effort at reconciliation. Divorced persons may re-marry in the faith and there is no difference in the wedding ceremony. The Baha'ís say that they would support and help separated members, and place great emphasis on pre-marriage counselling.

Baptists. Followers in Ireland: 9,000 (Republic 1,000)
The following is a personal response from Revd Robert Dunlop MA, pastor of the Baptist Church at Brannockstown, Kilcullen, Co. Kildare, for 30 years. These comments do not necessarily reflect the position of the Baptist Union of Ireland or the Southern Association of Irish Baptist Churches.
    Some Baptists have permitted divorce, mainly on the grounds of adultery and desertion as outlined in Biblical texts.

Consistent with our congregational form of church government, there is diversity on the subject within the Irish Baptist family of churches.

Personally, yes I will re-marry divorced persons provided I am satisfied pastorally that there is seriousness of intent on the part of the parties and that they affirm the permanent nature of the marriage contract. Failure to achieve a successful marriage is taken seriously, but not regarded as unpardonable.

While there is provision for a simplified service of 'blessing' for those who have been re-married in a civil ceremony, those who are getting married in a full church ceremony would enter the same vows as everyone else. I do not agree with divorced people being offered a 'watered-down' or 'reduced' form of service just because a previous marriage failed. They deserve the dignity of a new beginning – if the person performing the ceremony is uneasy about their stance or has reservations about the 'validity' of a new marriage, this should be made clear and other arrangements made.

There is a wide spectrum of opinion among Baptists, ranging from 'no church re-marriage of divorced persons' to a more open stance, which treats the matter pastorally and where provision is made for each case to be considered carefully and, if specific criteria are in place, which has no insuperable barrier to church re-marriage.

The *de facto* situation of many thousands of broken and irreparable marriages, and the social changes in society, will require a more tolerant stance. It is now understood that there are complexities to be faced and realism demands a generous approach on the part of Christian communities without loss of principle or conviction. There is little evidence of a loss of church members because of our position on marital breakdown.

Support for couples in difficulty would normally be provided through the pastoral arrangements of the local church, but this is an area which needs to be kept under review.

Baptists teach that as a Divine ideal, marriage is permanent. This is a theological statement. We also hold that the state has the responsibility to legislate for the well-being of all its citizens. Personally, I believe that there is an infringement of civil liberties where a substantial number of people are 'legally imprisoned' in marriage contracts when in fact the marriage is already dead. Provision for limited civil divorce is a necessity in modern Irish society. We see it as our responsibility to oppose legislation which would encourage divorce on

demand, or 'quickie' dissolutions. But there is a serious incon-
sistency in recognising foreign divorces without legislating
adequately for the domestic situation, and this anomaly
should be removed.

Church of Ireland. Followers in Southern Ireland: 96,000
While the Church of Ireland believes that marriage should be a
lifelong, monogamous union, they say that the civil law of
marriage is not intended to be a translation of the teachings of
Christ into legal terms, but a reflection of the community's own
view of the way in which marriage should be regulated in the
secular sphere. They made it clear in their submission to the
Joint Committee of the Oireachtas on Marriage Breakdown that
the introduction of a divorce law, unsatisfactory as it must
always be, was the best solution to the problem of marriage
breakdown which was available to civil law. The 1994 Synod has
now decided that legislation will be enacted which will enable a
divorced person to be married in the Church, providing an act of
penitence is made. This act of penitence is separate from the subsequent marriage ceremony.

Church of Jesus Christ of the Latter Day Saints (Mormons).
Followers in Ireland: 5,000-7,000
The Mormons believe in an eternal marriage and would counsel
people not to separate. They do, however, accept the decision of
individuals to separate, and would not expel someone from the
Church if they so decided. The Mormons will re-marry divorced
persons and their wedding ceremony is no different than that
for first-time marriages. They also have support groups for
single or separated parents.

Islam. Followers in Ireland: 6,000
The Islamic faith has always allowed divorce, although it is considered to be the most displeasing to God of all the permissible
acts. Divorce is allowed when it is not possible for a husband
and wife to live together, but the faith offers informal
conciliatory help for couples who are having marital problems.
Divorced persons can also remarry in the faith, and this is
normal practice in Muslim societies. The Islamic community in
Ireland considers the constitutional ban an infringement of their
rights.

Judaism. Followers in Ireland: 2,000
Divorce is allowed within the Jewish faith; in fact there is a document, called a ketuba, which the bride is given at the wedding and holds, which details what she will receive should the couple separate. If a divorced person wishes to re-marry within the faith, they are allowed to do so and there is a difference of only one word in the ceremony, referring to the fact that it is not the first marriage. Due to the closeness of the Jewish community in Ireland, friends give support in marital-breakdown situations, and people with problems normally go to their rabbi. When appropriate the Chief Rabbi refers people to the Marriage Counselling Service.

Lutheran Church. Followers in Ireland: 1,000 (however, the largest Protestant Church in world terms)
Divorce is allowed by Lutherans and re-marriage is allowed in the church, but the Pastor has the discretion to refuse to perform a ceremony. This can be appealed to the Bishop, and if re-marriage is granted against the Pastor's judgement he is not obliged to perform the ceremony. Pastor Paul Fritz, who responded to the questionnaire, stated that he felt that the absence of divorce was an infringement of civil rights, and that in present circumstances it would prevent him from applying for Irish citizenship. He also felt that, as the vast majority of their members in Ireland were non-Irish nationals, they found the whole legal/canonical problem of minor interest to them.

Presbyterian Church. Followers in Republic of Ireland: 12,000
While the Presbyterian Church has a special group counselling people experiencing marital difficulties, and feel that divorce should be only a last resort, they will remarry divorced persons. The wedding ceremony for divorced persons is no different from the normal religious ceremony. There is general agreement in the Church that a total ban on divorce is an infringement of their civil liberties.

The Quakers (Religious Society of Friends). Followers in Ireland: 1,600 approx.
The Quakers accept the law of the land in which they live; therefore they would recognise divorce if it were to be introduced in the Republic of Ireland, as they already do in the north of Ireland. In fact, one of the contributors to the pre-1937

constitution, which allowed divorce, was James Green Douglas, a Quaker. The Quaker wedding ceremony does not differentiate between divorced persons and first-time marriages. Because of their sympathetic attitude to various social problems, the Quakers feel that, especially in the south of Ireland, they have gained members who are disillusioned by more authoritarian religions.

Roman Catholic Church. Members in Ireland: 3.9 million
The Catholic Press and Information Office state that the marriage of baptised persons (see note), properly celebrated and consummated, is a sacrament, and that such a marriage is for life. Neither partner is ever free to contract a new marriage during the lifetime of the other. The only exception that the Roman Catholic church makes is in the area of nullity where, because of serious defects of consent or capacity, the marriage is found to be invalid. The onus is on the applicant to prove that a marriage should be annulled.

The Catholic Press and Information Office states that 'the church will not solemnise the sacrament of marriage unless both parties are free to marry; if one or both of the parties is already validly married, the church will not "remarry" them.'

Author's note: Church annulments, while based on strict grounds, are granted more often than state annulments. While they may, according to ecclesiastical law, state that a Roman Catholic marriage did not exist, they cannot grant the legal right to remarry. The practice in England is for the Church not to process annulments unless they have evidence of a decree absolute from the courts first.
Note: the questionnaire asked if each Church allows, or ever allowed divorce; the reply stated that there was no re-marriage of baptised persons. What was not stated is that the Pauline and Petrine privileges still apply. These allow a Roman Catholic who was formerly married to a non-Christian to remarry in the Roman Catholic church or, if a non-Christian converts and wishes to marry a Roman Catholic, any previous marriage to a non-Christian can be dissolved. While these are unusual cases, in 1981 the above accounted for 2,305 marriages worldwide. Up until the twelfth century, divorce was in fact granted by the Roman Catholic Church.

Creating Space for Debate:
The Catholic Church's contribution

Patrick Riordan SJ

Divorce is one of a series of major issues which have provoked heated public debate in Ireland in the past two decades. All who have participated in these debates know exactly how heated they can become. Emotions frequently run high because the issues at stake typically touch on people's fundamental religious and moral convictions, as well as on their own personal experience of pain and suffering. The slogans relied upon in public campaigning undoubtedly reflect these powerful emotions: 'Put compassion in the Constitution', 'Christ says no!' Will another debate on the issues of a Constitutional amendment to remove the ban on divorce legislation be equally heated and divisive? Or has experience taught people to conduct these debates in a reasoned and calm manner, and with a spirit of tolerance for those holding differing views?

SPACE FOR DEBATE

The many issues which have provoked this heated debate have been about law: changes to the criminal law such as decriminalising homosexual activity and legalising the public sale of contraceptives; and changes to the Constitution, such as seeking a guarantee of protection in law for unborn life, and the removal of the ban on divorce. What has made these debates about the law particularly heated has been the connection with moral issues. People are not used to having their moral standards called into question in debate; these standards they accept as the basis on which to consider concrete problems or, particularly, different issues. But in a debate on what the law should be, people must be capable of calling into question whether the law need be or should be as it has been received. People must be capable of a flexibility in relation to the law which one should not expect of them in relation to their own moral standards. Such a capacity presupposes an ability to distinguish in practice between law and morality. Debates on the law therefore require a space all of their own, a space removed from the distinctively moral. So my question is: are we in Ireland creating such a space for debate about the law as a result of our various attempts to handle the issues facing us? Is our political culture learning how to conduct public controversy and generate workable solutions on delicate matters?

It is frequently asserted that the Catholic Church is a major obstacle to the formation of a public space for debate in Ireland. Such a view is one-sided. A careful reading of official statements by the Irish Catholic hierarchy reveals that theirs has been one of the voices most clearly calling for an appropriate space. Now, of course what is said in the heat of debate or by particular individual representatives, or what is filtered by the media, is not always consistent with the official position. But that official position is in fact in favour of the kind of space for debate referred to above.

DEVELOPMENT IN THE CHURCH'S POSITION

The public debates on law and morality, as well as the New Ireland Forum, have given the Irish Catholic hierarchy the opportunity to clarify publicly their position in regard to the law. What comes ever more clearly out of these public statements is that the Church does not ask that her moral teaching be reflected in the law. For instance, in the pastoral letter Love Is for Life, the bishops do not hesitate to present the Church's moral teaching on marriage and divorce:

> For those, therefore, who accept the teaching of the Catholic Church, divorce with the right to remarry is not merely not permitted, it is impossible. No legislative enactment can dissolve a valid marriage and leave the partners free to marry again. (181)

But having presented this traditional teaching, the bishops make it clear that they do not draw any immediate implication from this teaching for the law of the country:

> The Catholic Church teaches that remarriage following divorce is impossible; but it does not follow from this alone that the laws of the State must embody this principle (185)... We do not ask that Catholic Doctrine be enshrined in law (187)...

In an Appendix to their pastoral letter, the bishops reproduced statements made in the context of the various debates. From their 1973 statement on proposals to change the law regarding contraceptives they insisted: 'Those who insist on seeing the issue purely in terms of the State enforcing Catholic moral teaching, are therefore missing the point' (94). Their submission to the New Ireland Forum, also quoted in the Appendix, stated the principle in general terms:

> The Catholic Church in Ireland totally rejects the concept of a confessional state. We have not sought and we do not seek a Catholic State for a Catholic people. (p.96)

I see this developing commitment by the hierarchy to a distinction between the spheres of morality and of law as a significant contribution to the creation of a space for public debate. This development is the product of a learning process in the Church, stimulated by the shift in approach taken by the Second Vatican Council in its discussion of the grounds for religious liberty. The Council, in its Declaration on Religious Liberty, insisted that:

> All should be immune from coercion on the part of individuals, social groups and every human power, so that, within due limits, nobody is forced to act against his convictions nor is anyone to be restrained from acting in accordance with his convictions in religious matters, in private or in public, alone or in association with others.

Patrick Hannon, in his book *Church, State, Morality and Law*, argues that this principle, which was articulated for the right to religious liberty, becomes a guiding principle for other aspects of social life. In other words, just as the State, through its laws, should not attempt to coerce people, positively or negatively, in matters of religious belief and practice, so also should it not attempt to restrict or coerce people in matters which affect their freedom of action in accordance with their own conscience.

Does this imply that those who decide on divorce should not be restricted by law from exercising their freedom? The Council does not go so far. There is a qualification, hinted at above in the quoted phrase 'within due limits'. The exercise of freedom should not be hindered, according to the same Declaration, except when and in so far as is necessary for 'the just requirements of public order', of peace, justice and public morality. But what is required for the maintenance of public order and justice is not immediately evident. It is precisely here that the space for debate arises out of legitimate disagreement. Politicians and voters are faced with the challenge of forming an opinion on what is most conduvice to public order, and on the limits to be imposed on individuals' liberty for the sake of that common good.

In matters of law and morality, therefore, those with the responsibility of making the law must not ask, 'What is moral?' but 'What is best for public order and public morality?' This is the official position of the Irish bishops. And it amounts to the insistence that there be another space, a separate forum, for debates about the law, even when they concern moral matters.

BISHOPS USING THE SPACE

Now, of course, everyone is aware that the bishops, while distinguishing between the questions of morality and those concerning the law, do not confine their contribution to the moral. They too have formed an opinion on what is good for public order, and do not hesitate to present it, although they always underline the kinds of reasons they rely on as different from their moral teaching. They address their arguments to voters and legislators precisely in their capacity as citizens and legislators with responsibility for the stability and public order of society and its basic institutions.

Would the introduction of divorce legislation in the Republic of Ireland contribute to public order and stabiliy in society, or would it be more likely to undermine them? The bishops adopt the latter position. They do not argue in terms of the nature of marriage or of marriage vows; they do not argue from authority; and they explicitly rule out a deduction from the wrongness of divorce on the moral level to its inappropriateness on the legal level. Instead, they base their arguments either on experience or on prognoses of the likely consequences of changes in the law (*Love Is for Life*, 190-212). They review arguments made in terms of the effect of a divorce law on the stability of marriage as an institution; the resulting change in the legal definition of marriage; the possible effects in terms of increased suffering for women and children; as well as noting the experience of other countries with divorce law. But the appeal to experience is not unambiguous, and prognoses are based on informed guesses: there is real possibility of disagreement in interpreting statistics, and intelligent observers can offer contradictory prognoses. The bishops are aware of this: they are aware of the differences in the interpretation of experience among serious and responsible commentators, and they are aware of the inconclusive nature of all prognoses.

It is on the basis of such expressions in their official position that I put forward the argument that the Irish hierarchy is committed to the creation and fostering of a distinct place in Irish public culture for debate about the law.

THE SPACE UNDERMINED IN PRACTICE

The reasons why the Irish bishops think that divorce would not be good for the quality of Irish public life were brought once again to public attention recently by the Archbishop of Dublin, Dr Desmond Connell. Preaching at a Mass in Knock to participants in the Dublin Diocesan Pilgrimage, the Archbishop warned that a law permitting divorce would undermine the foundation on which Irish family tradition depends. He said that society would promote its own disintegration by removing the requirement in law of life-long fidelity in marriage.

Because of this anticipated effect of divorce law on the institution of marriage and on society itself, he characterised divorce as radically anti-social. The Archbishop's strong statement was reported widely in the media. His sermon contained nothing new, but echoed the reasons explored by the hierarchy in their pastoral letter *Love Is for Life*. And yet I can understand the reaction of one member of the congregation at Knock who wrote to the *Irish Times* expressing her dismay that the Archbishop had chosen the occasion of a liturgy involving many sick and handicapped people seeking 'peace and healing' to make what she calls 'a statement on society'. She suggested that the Archbishop and other bishops should call public meetings when issuing press statements, but that their priority when preaching should be to minister to the needs of people.

The discordance between Dr Connell's intention and his listener's response is understandable in terms of the tension between the two aspects of the divorce issue as a question of morality, and as a question for society and its law. In so far as there is a moral question, the teaching authorities in the Church will communicate its teaching to believers through their appropriate channels, including sermons and homilies in the liturgy. But in so far as there is a question facing citizens and legislators, the appropriate channels are the public ones, including the media. The making of arguments about the social consequences of divorce in the context of a forum suited to the teaching of the faith leads to a confusion which undermines the very distinction the Irish bishops have taken great pains to introduce into the discussion. The ensuing confusion is that Catholics are unsure whether they are being asked to vote against divorce legislation because it is required of them by their faith – 'Christ says no', or because they are convinced by arguments based on experiences of divorce and on reasonable prognoses of anticipated consequences of its introduction. These reasons are of course the relevant ones, and they belong in the appropriate space for public debate which is gradually being created in Irish political culture.

The considerable achievement by the Irish bishops in contributing to the creation of that space by their official statements is put in jeopardy when the distinguished two levels are confused in practice.

THE SPACE DENIED

The confusion of the two levels is a risk not only for those on the anti-divorce side of the debate. *Debating Divorce: Moral Conflict in Ireland*, by Michele Dillon, an Irish sociologist teaching at Rutgers University, tries to understand the arguments in the divorce debate and hopes to explain why the proposal was defeated in the 1986 referendum.

In the course of the 1986 debate, two important distinctions were established: the distinction between the moral and the legal, and the distinction between Constitutional law and other law. As Dillon very adequately documents, the first distinction was made by various participants, including Garret FitzGerald, but, most significantly, by the Irish Episcopal Conference in their pastoral letter, *Love Is for Life.* Dillon records faithfully how the bishops (a) presented their views on divorce as a moral issue; (b) insisted that there was no direct implication from the moral position on divorce to what the law on marriage and divorce should be; and (c) offered reasons why they considered a divorce law would have negative consequences for Irish society. (92-5) From these considered statements, it is clear that the debate leading up to the referendum was to be about law, and not about the morality of divorce.

It would have been interesting had Dillon investigated the extent to which participants in the debate adopted this distinction and consistently applied it. Rather, instead of reviewing the debate as a debate about what the law should be, Dillon treats it throughout as a moral debate, as the subtitle of her book indicates.

Although Dillon faithfully reports the bishops' position, especially on (b) above, she none the less accuses them of presenting an economic and social case against divorce law, something which, as we have seen, they object to for purely moral reasons. The bishops are said to appropriate sociology in order 'to legitimise their traditional Catholic dogma'! (107). Arguments are made in 'this worldly', economic and social terms, but, she maintains, the real reasons behind this are 'other-worldly, moral and religious arguments' (149f). Both the bishops and the Anti-Divorce Campaign (ADC) are accused of contradictory discourse because of the confusion of these two levels.

A worrying aspect of this analysis is the way in which Dillon refuses to take participants at their word when they discuss divorce as a legal/social matter and not as a moral matter. She records, for instance, how successfully the two main spokespersons for the ADC, William Binchy and Joe McCarroll, confined their contributions in the debate to the likely negative consequences of divorce for society – ie the economic, social and legal considerations – and refused to be sidetracked by interviewers into statements on the morality of divorce (134). None the less she repeatedly asserts that their espoused positions were derived from moral stances which they would not admit, and that these moral stances were based on values which were irrational and not susceptible to argument. (149)

The other distinction which became crucial in the shaping of the debate was that between Constitutional and other law. The referendum asked the electorate to replace one article of the Constitution, which excluded law permitting divorce, with another article which would allow the legislature to provide for divorce. Though the debate was provoked by this proposal to change the Constitution, the main focus of argument was on the kind of divorce law the government intended to introduce. The opponents of the amendment very effectively set the agenda by asking for details of the proposed law, for example the provisions with regard to the wife and family of a first marriage, the sale of a matrimonial home, et cetera. The result is that the 1986 debate was in effect turned into a debate about the proposed law on divorce, rather than on the Constitutional amendment. It was a debate which the Government and the pro-divorce lobby lost, because – according to Dillon – they relied on the wording of the Constitutional amendment to outline divorce law and had neither details of a proposed law nor answers to detailed objections about issues such as social-welfare entitlements. All they seemed to offer were vague promises that their legislation, when eventually finalised, would deal with the issues raised by objectors. Dillon's study documents this, but fails to adopt the relevant distinction in her own analysis, and persists in speaking of the debate as a moral debate and not as a social and legal one.

Dillon's work amounts to an attack on this space for debate secured by a distinction between morality and law. Her insistence on treating the debate as one based on moral rather than legal considerations has the effect of disenfranchising a whole group of participants, whose arguments are not taken seriously because they are assumed to mean something other than what they say. This stance is inconsistent with the maintenance of a space in which citizens of competing and opposed viewpoints can meet in mutual respect and tolerance, and attempt to find some solution through reasonable argument.

CONCLUSION: WE MUST SECURE THE SPACE

The space required for public debate about the law is not to be taken for granted. It needs to be sustained and protected. The need for this space has become evident in recent controversies. The Catholic Church, being a major voice in many of these debates, has also contributed significantly to the definition of the space needed for debates about the law. However, the Church is also in danger of violating this space when it seems to confuse in practice its two roles of teaching Catholic faith and presenting its social analysis. The space is violated also by those who refuse to take seriously arguments of a social or economic nature, and, instead of meeting them with corresponding counter-arguments, accuse their opponents of unfair play.

The space for debate about the law – that is, the space for considering what contributes to and what undermines public order, the stability of society, security and justice – is precarious.

REFERENCES
1. Dillon, Michele *Debating Divorce. Moral Conflict in Ireland*. Lexington: The University Press of Kentucky, 1993.
2. Cf. Flannery, Austin ed. Vatican Council II: Conciliar and Post Conciliar Documents. New York: Costello, 1975, p.800.
3. Hannan, Patrick *Church, State, Morality and Law*. Dublin: Gill and Macmillan, 1992, Chapter 7.
4. Cf. *Irish Times*, Monday 16 May 1994, p.4.
5. *Irish Times*, Saturday 21 May, Letters to the Editor.
6. *Love Is for Life*. Irish Bishops' Pastoral, Dublin, Veritas: 1985. References in parentheses to paragraph numbers.

Separating and Coping Alone or in a Second Relationship

Mags O'Brien and others

The following chapter covers some of the many practical problems that people face if they separate. The ones covered here are those that have been cited to us over the last year, in phone calls and visits to our office, or raised by members. The second half of this chapter lists information and support groups.

If you feel that your marriage is in troubled waters, the most important thing for each of you to do is to communicate with each other; lack of communication is one of the biggest killers of relationships. If you can't resolve your differences together, look for counselling. Of course, sometimes this is not possible, as one partner may have already left or may refuse to seek help. Perhaps the most important thing to do is to ask for advice early and often. Community centres and citizens' advice bureaux will assist you in getting information on your rights. They will also give you information on applications for medical cards and for rent allowance or mortgage relief. Don't feel too proud to look for help: it is vital that you ensure that you don't get into debt because of your pride. Problems, especially money problems, become bigger if you ignore them.

If you feel able to do so, join a group such as the Separated Persons Association or Gingerbread, and get information from those who have been down the road before you. These groups are also a source of support; separated people can feel very isolated, especially as they tend to lose some of the friends they had as part of a couple. While it's great to have one good friend, don't overload that person; share your troubles with friends and family.

Talking is often the best medicine. Try not to paint your partner as totally black, because if you manage to reconcile your differences you will feel foolish telling everyone that you really that want them back, despite all you have said. Also, be aware of little ears. It is vitally important to discuss a separation with children, but it is equally important not to burden them with having to take sides.

COUNSELLING

If a couple are experiencing problems in their marriage, they may decide to look for counselling. The voluntary groups AIM and Gingerbread provide a counselling service, and the largest counselling body is the Catholic Marriage Advisory Council (CMAC), which has branches countrywide. While the religious ethos of the CMAC may be off-putting to some, those who have attended found that in the main they were sympathetically received whatever their own religious background. There is also a non-denominational counselling service, Marriage Counselling Service Ltd, 24 Grafton Street Dublin 2.

If a partner's excessive drinking is the cause of marital discord, Al-Anon will give support to the family.

On many occasions, however, counselling is not practicable either because of violence or desertion, or because of the refusal of one partner to attend.

SEPARATION

No two separations happen in exactly the same way, and for every couple there will be different issues to handle and different ways of handling them. Much may depend on the reason for the breakdown of the marriage. Obviously, the sudden departure of a spouse will impact differently than a more gradual breakdown. The presence of children also dictates the avenues taken to formalise separation.

Contrary to popular belief, it is often months or years before many couples formalise a *de facto* breakdown, possibly because one partner still hopes for reconciliation or, more often, because informal arrangements have evolved. After a certain length of time most parting couples do, however, decide to formalise the separation, for either financial or emotional reasons.

In the past it would have been normal for each party to consult their own solicitor when separating. Whether the case would go to court or could be settled by negotiation would depend very much on the advice they received and the level of acrimony between them. The problem with the adversarial system, however, has always been that the perceived duty of each solicitor or barrister is to get the best deal for their client, regardless of whether this is the fairest deal for the whole family or the one least likely to reduce future acrimony.

MEDIATION

Mediation has evolved as an alternative to the problematic adversarial method of resolving differences. Mediation relies on individuals to behave as adults and empowers them to negotiate their own agreements. Agreements that are reached in such a manner are far less likely to break down than those imposed by the court system, because the participants feel that their wishes have been addressed as far as possible.

The State Mediation Service, set up as a pilot scheme by the government in September 1986, has recently been put on a permanent footing. The service is based in the Irish Life Centre in Dublin and demand is high, with waiting lists of three months or more. AIM and Gingerbread also provide a limited mediation service. The state service is free, and AIM and Gingerbread are paid for by voluntary contribution. There are also a number of private mediators, and details of these can be obtained from the Mediators Institute, 30 Fortfield Park, Terenure, Dublin 6.

The difficulty of travelling to Dublin for several sessions puts free mediation out of reach of many, and although the Minister for Equality has given a commitment to expand the state service, there are as yet no concrete plans for such expansion.

According to Maura Wall-Murphy of the Family Mediation Service: 'The four areas that people normally want to deal with and make decisions on are the family home, finance, children and property. Statistics of the first 200 couples who attended the service showed that almost half cited all four issues as needing mediation and most spouses gave more than one issue. Depending on the issues, the mediator may tell the couple to seek legal advice before proceeding further.'

The Rules of Family Mediation

- Mediation is a process where parties in dispute, with the aid of a mediator, negotiate their own agreement.
- Mediation offers an alternative to the adversarial legal system. It differs from arbitration, marriage counselling and therapy in important ways. Mediation is not a legal advice service. The principle underlying mediation is that couples take responsibility for resolving their own disputes as opposed to having decisions made for them by a third party, as in arbitration.
- Mediation can work only if entered into freely and with the

participation of both parties.
- All issues arising from the dispute are open for negotiation. In marital separation these include parenting, living arrangements, family home, financial support, property, and the education, health and welfare of the children.
- All discussions arising out of mediation are confidential and the mediator will not voluntarily disclose any information obtained through the mediation process except with the consent of all affected parties, or when releasing non-identifying information for research or education.
- The mediator does not take sides or testify voluntarily in court on behalf of either party.
- The mediator promotes the balanced interests of the whole family.
- To ensure that participants make decisions based on sufficient information, it is important that a full and frank disclosure is made of all financial and other relevant information.
- It is advisable for each party to take to their respective solicitors the agreement prepared in mediation to have it formalised before signing and, where appropriate, to seek outside consultation on long-term tax and legal consequences of different proposals.
- In the event of a breakdown in the agreement or any change in circumstances affecting the agreement, the parties will return to mediation to re-negotiate the issues in question.
- Either party or the mediator has the right to suspend or withdraw from mediation at any time.

Obviously any mediated agreement remains unofficial, and therefore it is necessary to consult a solicitor to have it stamped. However, solicitors are reluctant to act for both parties on a mediated agreement and therefore will normally insist that each spouse has separate representation. While this may be more costly, they fear that one partner to the agreement may later become disgruntled and accuse them of favouring the other party.

While the Law Society's recommended fee for a straightforward separation agreement is approximately £350, obviously those consulting a solicitor with a mediated agreement are less likely to incur higher costs because they will have ironed out disputed areas without the solicitor's clock ticking.

SOLICITORS

If mediation is not possible or practicable, it is important to look for a solicitor who has experience in family law. While the Law Society and the Family Lawyers Association have listings, not all of the solicitors on these lists deal with family law on a regular basis. Perhaps the best way to find a reliable solicitor is to talk to others who have been through the process.

LEGAL AID

If finances do not permit the services of a solicitor, a means-tested free legal-aid service exists. Funding for this is totally inadequate, with waiting lists of three to nine months, depending on the legal-aid centre. Contacts for these centres are listed in the Appendix to this book, and groups such as FLAC and AIM also give advice in family law.

SEPARATION AGREEMENTS

Where a couple mutually agree on the terms of a separation or have mediated an agreement, then they can have the agreement stamped as a legal document. Solicitors will not do this without both parties having had independent legal advice, which unfortunately increases the cost. As with any consultation, be sure to ask beforehand what the costs will be.

CUSTODY

In common with other countries, it seems that in the vast majority of marital-breakdown situations, the Irish courts award custody of the children to their mother. With the increased involvement of fathers in parenting, this trend is changing slightly, with a move in some countries towards joint custody. The concept of joint custody does not actually exist in Irish law, but increasingly judges are beginning to make orders stating that children must spend some time in each parent's care. In these situations, both parents are the child's legal guardians, and, as such, the non-custodial parent should be consulted on issues such as education, et cetera. As stated in Chapter 5, enforced joint-custody orders may, however, be problematic, as resentment arises if decisions are not jointly arrived at.

According to AIM statistics, 19 per cent of clients seeking information in 1994 and 22 per cent in 1993 had queries relating to custody. The Contact centre in Finglas states that 7.5 per cent of their clients looked for information concerning their children. It appears that in acrimonious breakdown situations, threats are sometimes made by one party to deny the other access to or custody of the children. It must be understood that people are hurt and grieving in such situations and may act vindictively or irrationally because of grief and anger. (Obviously cases of alleged child abuse may be exceptions, but great care should be taken with these.) What is not clear, because no statistical data exist, is how many people have stayed in a relationship because of the fear that they would lose the children if they left. Some women who have left the family home because of violence have given the reason for their later return as the fear that they will in fact lose the children, especially if the husband has good standing in the community.

When the issue of custody is becoming contentious, mediation can help with this, as it seems from case histories that custody arrangements that are mutually agreed by parents and children (if the children are old enough to understand) are less likely to run into trouble. If the separation itself is a bitter one, then the issue of custody may be used, consciously or unconsciously, as a blunt instrument in bargaining. It is noticeable and tragic that disputes over custody are far rarer and less bitter where the couples do not have property or investments – a trend that is confirmed by AIM and other counselling centres.

The issue of custody has been addressed in some countries by separating it from the other issues to be decided on divorce, precisely so that it is not used as a bargaining point. The real question to be asked in all custody cases is what is in the best interest of the child(ren) involved.

Many organisations have stressed that family tribunals are the preferred way to tackle custody problems, and that judges are not necessarily well placed to decide on the suitablity or otherwise of either parent. These would have the advantage that they would be less formal than courts, improving the position of the less advantaged parent in cases where custody is the subject of bitter dispute.

The present wording of the Judicial Separation Act states that the judge must decide custody with due regard to, amongst other areas the religious, financial and moral welfare of the child(ren). This leaves room for all sorts of accusations and counter-accusations about the 'fitness' or otherwise of a parent. Unless someone has led a totally blameless life, any past problems will be magnified in an effort to blacken characters on both sides in custody cases. This may be particularly worrying for anyone who has, for example, had an alcohol problem in the past or has undergone treatment for mental illness. Problems also occur if the partner seeking to retain custody has had an affair or is currently cohabiting with a third party; sexual orientation is also used as a ground to contest custody. Celebrity cases such as that of Woody Allen and Mia Farrow spring to mind when addressing this issue. This can result in lengthy psychological testing of parents and children. The question can become very difficult if one parent has allegedly abused the child(ren). The court may order supervised access only of this parent to the child, or may deny access altogether.

One spouse may apply for a custody order on her/his own, free of charge, but where there is a possibility of acrimony it is highly advisable to have the services of a solicitor. Naturally, the cost of these can make this process prohibitively expensive for a parent on a low income, often the woman, particularly if the opposing spouse has the financial resources to pay for his own legal advice. Any separating person in this situation should consult their local Citizens Advice Centre for information on free legal aid.

The longer a case goes on, the stronger the position of the parent with custody, as the courts are reluctant to uproot a child. Again it has to be stressed that the child's wellbeing should be the main consideration. It is also important that both parents continue to parent, wherever possible, and agreed custody is the best way to achieve this.

As mentioned above, another cause of concern in the area of custody is that, on separation, one parent (usually the woman), may have no independent means and therefore cannot afford a solicitor. While they may resort to free legal aid, the reality is that the Legal Aid Board is overburdened; therefore, no matter how well qualified their staff, not enough of their time can be devoted to giving specific attention to any one case.

There have also been numerous incidents of cross-border 'tug of love' cases where the legal-aid services have been unable to provide support in other countries, leaving the parent in Ireland scared and vulnerable, and unable to take legal action in the country to which their children have been taken. Obviously such cases should receive more attention from the Department of Foreign Affairs, and if necessary, financial support in finding solicitors in the country where the case is being heard should be given. There seems to be a marked reluctance by Foreign Affairs to intervene where the child(ren) are not presently resident in Ireland, even though many countries involved are now covered by the Hague and Luxembourg Conventions, which give recognition to custody orders granted in signatory states. The Hague convention also allows for expeditious procedures for the return of a child – procedures which can operate in the absence of a court order from the state in which the child was removed. (White Paper:1992)

While, in the majority of cases, the issue of custody is eventually resolved, it may, because it can drag on for months or, in some cases, years, add to the trauma that always comes with marital breakdown. What does appear, as mentioned before, is that in most cases where custody becomes an issue, it is because one partner is using it as a lever to negotiate financial settlements. Again, the use of mediation can be of great help here, but in the final analysis, the question is: what is best for the children, and do judges have the necessary training to decide that?

FOREIGN DIVORCES

Due to the absence of divorce in Ireland, many separating people seek divorces in other countries. While most couples in second relationships are aware that many such divorces are not recognised here, they feel that going though the motions of getting one helps them to put an end to an often sad chapter of their lives. Some may also decide to go through a wedding ceremony in a registry office outside Ireland. This is of particular significance to those who have children in their second family, and for many it emphasises their commitment to each other. Some also feel that it legitimises their relationship in the eyes of their own parents and family.

In some cases foreign divorces are valid, and the 1994 Family

Law Bill is set to allow for the application to Irish courts for financial relief. (Prior to this there was no mechanism here for anyone who was legally divorced in another country to obtain maintenance et cetera.)

Types of foreign divorce
There are two distinct types of foreign divorces.

Firstly, the obviously 'dodgy' ones, for instance one obtained by a separated Irish couple who live in Ireland but use an English address to obtain a divorce.

To obtain a divorce in England or Wales it is necessary that the applicant has resided in there for a year; otherwise the decree is invalid. Obviously, if the divorce isn't valid, a subsequent marriage will not be recognised in Ireland either (although the Revenue Commissioners may accept the new marriage certificate for tax purposes).

The second type of foreign divorce is that obtained when one of the parties resides outside Ireland. Most people are of the impression that the Recognition of Foreign Divorce Act (1986) means that such divorces are recognised in Ireland. The reality is that, due to the wording of the legislation and subsequent court challenges, it is extremely difficult to prove that a foreign divorce should be recognised in this country. Because of the protection for marriage enshrined in our Constitution, Irish law relating to matrimony takes a narrow and restrictive view on the question of domicile (where you live).

Foreign divorces are recognised without question only when the person obtaining the divorce is not Irish and obtained the divorce in their own country while residing there.

What does domicile really mean in Irish law?
Domicile is defined in this instance as either *domicile of origin*, normally taken to mean where you were born, but really determined by the domicile of a controlling parent; or *domicile of choice*, ie that you moved to another jurisdiction and set up permanent residence there. So why, then, is there a problem?

Let's take the case of Mary and John. They separate; Mary subsequently moves to England and, after a year's residence, obtains a divorce there. While the English authorities will recognise her divorce as valid, the Irish authorities say that John must prove that Mary intends to stay in England if he wants to remarry. It is not enough to prove that she is now resident there; she must have made a choice to stay there. In practice more than one piece of evidence is necessary; even buying a house and setting up a business may not be seen as sufficient proof.

A further difficulty would arise if Mary and John were not on speaking terms, because she might refuse to give him any assistance in proving her domicile. If a person wishes to remarry the law requires him to prove that there is no reason why they should not be able to do so.

While this seems an extremely harsh interpretation of the law by the Registrars Office, the registrars are bound by Irish legislation as determined by various Supreme Court judgements, for example *MTT v NTT*.

The jurisdiction in which a divorce is obtained can also cause problems. Section 5 of the Recognition of Foreign Divorces Act states that if countries have more than one jurisdiction, each of those jurisdictions is classified as separate, and the general rules of domicile apply. Thus an Irish court would not recognise a divorce obtained in California by someone who ordinarily resides in Philadelphia. This also applies to pre-1986 divorces obtained in any of the UK's three jurisdictions, England and Wales, Scotland, and Northern Ireland. Australia, on the other hand, has only one jurisdiction.

SECOND RELATIONSHIPS
The lack of divorce legislation means that those in second relationships are faced with many problems. The areas of social welfare and pensions are addressed in other chapters of this book.

REGISTRATION OF BIRTHS
If a couple have a child and the mother has been married before (and her first partner is still alive), it is not possible to register the baby in hospital. It must be registered instead at the local office of the Registrar of Births, Deaths and Marriages. At present the mother must have proof that her ex-husband is not the father of her child. This proof may be in the form of a separation agreement or some other evidence that she has not co-habited with her husband for nine months prior to the birth. If

such proof is not available, she must obtain a declaration from her ex-husband. If the mother wishes to have the father's name on the certificate, the couple should go to a peace commissioner or notary and make a declaration that both agree to his name being registered.

A father's name on a birth certificate does not give him an automatic right of guardianship, and, while this will not normally pose problems, it is still advisable for the father to initiate guardianship proceedings. This can be done by the parents, and no solicitor is needed. An application should be made to the Clerk of the Family Court for a hearing, which takes only a few minutes.

Attitudes to Registration

There have been numerous complaints about the bureaucracy of registration. It seems that rules are arbitrary and that there is an insensitivity in handling some cases. One example is that of a woman whose separation agreement was in her married name (as is frequently the case). She had since reverted to her own name and the registrar insisted on recording her as follows 'Mary Murphy, formerly Jones, now Murphy'! In effect this meant that her ex-husband's name appeared on the birth certificate of her child.

When separation agreements containing financial and other arrangements are produced, they are frequently copied by the registrar and put on file. However, sight of such documents or a copy of the page showing the date of separation should be sufficient. If you are unhappy or uncomfortable about the treatment you receive, ask to see a supervisor.

BANKS AND CREDIT CARDS

There have been complaints in the past about the policies of those issuing credit cards: for instance, AIB Visa will not allow a cohabiting couple to open an account in both names, although Bank of Ireland, Ulster Bank and National Irish Bank do. (AIB say that the main cardholder must be related to, or in business with, the second person in order that they assume liability for their debts; the other banks take the view that, if the main cardholder permits a secondary card on their account, they are assuming responsibility for any debts the other cardholder may incur.)

Many separated women, even when working, have also had difficulties in obtaining loans; it seems that banks and lending agencies operate discriminatory practices. If you feel you have been unfairly refused a loan, you should ask for an explanation in writing and take the case up with the customer service department of the institution. You may also take your case to the Ombudsman; however, women frequently find that because of their other responsibilities they do not have the time to pursue such courses. Remember that if you are being unfairly treated you can always take your custom away.

What is the Position of the Church on Foreign Divorces and Second Marriages?

As stated earlier, the position of the Roman Catholic Church in Ireland adds to the confusion surrounding second marriages. In some instances, where a civil marriage has taken place outside Ireland and a divorce has later been granted, people think that they can marry again in the Catholic Church in Ireland. The reality is that, unless the state recognises their divorce or has granted a state annulment, such a marriage is bigamous. When performing a wedding the priest is acting for the state, and, contrary to popular opinion, a church wedding is legally binding even if the register is not signed. (This stipulation applies only to Roman Catholics, as other religions have to obtain licences or a registrar's certificate prior to marrying.)

Annulments

Legal annulments are costly and the grounds on which they may be granted are extremely narrow. In practice only between twenty and thiry annulments a year are granted.

In the past the main grounds for annulments were non-consummation of the marriage, or lack of mental capacity of one of the partners. Recent judgements have been broadened to include broader grounds such duress, but the numbers granted are still extremely small.

A state annulment dissolves a marriage – effectively declaring that it never existed – and therefore, once an annulments has been obtained, the parties are free to enter into a second civil marriage. Before the 1987 Status of Children Act, however, which effectively removed the legal status of illegitimacy, any children of the annulled marriage were illegitimate, with all the legal disadvantages that entailed at the time.

CHURCH ANNULMENT

The grounds for Church annulments are similar to those for state annulments, but Church annulments are more frequently granted. They have no legality whatsoever and do not entitle either party to remarry. It should be noted that a priest officiating at a wedding where one of the partners has a Church annulment but no state-recognised divorce is actually breaking the law; the Roman Catholic Church holds a privileged position and priests are recognised as registrars. It is imperative that anyone who has been through such a second 'marriage' takes legal advice to ensure that they are properly protected in the event of the death of their present partner.

PROBATE TAX

At the moment probate tax is not payable if you are survived by a spouse, but this does not apply to second relationships, where tax of two per cent would be payable except on estates of less than £10,000 (index-linked), and on money paid for funeral expenses. Obviously separate arrangements must be made for cohabiting couples

Property held in joint names or property that does not pass under the will or on intestacy is not subject to this two per cent charge.

When a person dies without leaving a will, intestacy rules apply. Under these rules a legal spouse inherits two thirds of the estate, while children share the remaining third equally. If there are no children, the legal spouse takes all.

The term 'legal right' refers to a spouse's legal right to a share of the estate left by a person who has made a will. Regardless of the contents of the will itself, the legal spouse is entitled to a third of the estate if the deceased is survived by a child; if the deceased leaves no children, the legal spouse is entitled to half the estate. The rest of the estate passes in accordance with the will. Children have no automatic entitlement to anything from a parent's estate.

TAX RELIEF

Double tax relief is presently not available to cohabiting couples; however, the Department of Social Welfare is presently addressing this issue. Interestingly, the Revenue Commissioners accept a foreign wedding certificate for tax purposes, so while the registrar may not recognise your divorce, the taxman will recognise your subsequent marriage!

CAPITAL ACQUISITIONS TAX

Capital acquisitions tax is charged on both gifts and inheritances. There is no CAT on gifts and inheritances between spouses; however, there is a threshold of £10,000 (index-linked) on gifts from a cohabitee; gifts or inheritances in excess of this value will be subject to tax. The values of any gifts/inheritances received after 2 June 1982 are added together for this purpose. In other words, if you received an inheritance from a parent, and your unofficial partner signed half their house over to you, the value of the two 'gifts' is combined, and the £10,000 exemption taken from the total.

PENSIONS (SEE ALSO CHAPTER ON PENSIONS)

It is important that anyone who has separated, and those in second relationships, should be fully aware of the rules of their pension schemes. It may be necessary to take out additional cover and it is vital that advice is obtained from a reputable broker or your solicitor.

Present Rules

At present these are the rules that apply to most schemes.

Private Schemes: in general the trustees have discretion about who receives the benefit from schemes.

Public Service Schemes: only the legal (cohabiting) spouse can receive the benefit; however the lump sum can go to the estate. (Many schemes vary because of the fact that up until 1981 women could opt out of the widows/orphans part of scheme).

What are the implications for those in subsequent relationships?

Private Schemes: settlement is at the discretion of the trustees, who usually feel that they have a duty to exercise their discretion and review each case on its individual merits. Lump sums may be paid into estates and, if there is a financial dependency at the time of death, they may grant the pension to the cohabiting partner. If the previous spouse was deemed to be dependent, the trustees may decide to divide the pension between the spouse and the second partner. If a previous spouse was mentioned as a beneficiary in the pension agreement, and this was not subsequently altered, a court order may be necessary to change the beneficiary.

The use of a 'wishes' letter is most important here. A wishes letter states what you wish to happen to your pension/lump sum in the event of your death. This letter should be given to the trustees of your pension scheme, and it is most important that they are notified of any separation.

Public Service Schemes: as there is no common-law status in Ireland, partners who are in subsequent relationships are not entitled to pension benefit.

The wording of most schemes lists spouses, but does not make any reference to cohabitation. If cohabitation is mentioned in the scheme, then the legal spouse may not be entitled to get the pension. As stated previously, the lump sum can be paid to the estate, providing a wishes letter has been submitted.

WHAT SHOULD SEPARATING COUPLES DO ABOUT PENSIONS, PROPERTY ET CETERA?

Seek legal advice from a family-law solicitor and also from a reputable insurance broker. Do not put off making a will. If you are in a second relationship and if finances permit, it is advisable for your partner to take out an insurance policy on you and vice versa. This ensures some protection for your partner and children.

If you have children from a second relationship it is also advisable to appoint guardians and to ensure that both estates (yours and your partner's) will placed in trust should you die while the children are under age. In order that there is no ambiguity about home ownership in the event of the death of either partner, it may be necessary to buy the new family home as an investment property and pay the tax accordingly.

LOCAL AUTHORITY HOUSING

The availability of local authority housing for separated persons depends to a great extent on the county/district in which they live. It is often difficult for the partner who has to leave the family home to obtain local authority housing if they do not have children. In Dublin social problems have arisen from a policy of grouping separated/lone parents in the same housing area, meaning that there is no societal mix and that the people there are effectively 'ghettoised'. If you require housing, a visit to your local TD's clinic is, sadly, often the best way of furthering your case.

VIOLENT RELATIONSHIPS

Those contemplating leaving an violent relationship face extra problems. The option of mediation is usually not open to them unless the offender has undergone counselling for their problem. Women in such situations may have to leave the home in the middle of the night to avoid further beatings.

The following contribution from Roisin McDermott, Chairwoman of Women's Aid, explains the rights and options of those contemplating leaving a violent situation.

Are You Being Abused?

Being battered means living in a situation where you or those for whom you care (your children or relatives) are being verbally, physically, mentally, emotionally and/or sexually abused. You don't have to be beaten to be battered.

Do you Feel you Have to Stay?

There are lots of pressures which make many women feel that there is nothing they can do about their situation and that they have to stay in an abusive relationship. For instance, many women think their children will suffer if they leave; have no money, support or help; think there is nowhere they can go; are afraid they will lose their family home; love their partner and keep hoping he will change; are afraid, ashamed or embarrassed; feel that 'he' has a right to do it; think it is all their own fault.

BUT: no man, in any circumstances, has the right to hit or abuse you; you and your children have the right to live in safety and peace in your own home.

There are things you can do to protect yourself and your

children, and people who can advise and offer you the practical and emotional support you need to change your situation.

What You Can Do

Contact the Women's Aid Helpline from 10.00 am to 10.00 pm from Monday to Friday. (Saturdays 10.00 am to 6.00 pm.) This is a freephone number, 1800 341900. The staff are specially trained to give you information, support and advice on any legal, social-welfare or housing queries you may have. The volunteers can offer you options/information which will help to guide you in making a decision about your future.

Your Rights

If you do not have sufficient income to pay for a private solicitor, you can apply for legal aid. The Women's Aid Helpline will give you the number in your local area.

Income

Every woman is entitled to a basic income of her own. You and your children have a right to receive Supplementary Welfare Allowance from the Community Welfare Officer at your local health centre. When you have been away from your husband for three months, you can apply for Lone Parent Allowance.

Housing

You and your children have the right to a family home. You have rights to your family home. If you have to leave because of violence, it is 'constructive desertion' on the part of your husband, and you do not lose these rights. If you wish to be re-housed by a local authority, you are eligible for housing as a one-parent family.

Seeking refuge/shelter

You and your children can seek shelter at the nearest women's refuge. The Women's Aid Helpline, 1800 341900, and the Women's Refuge, (01) 4961002 (24 hours), will help you find accommodation. (See listing for Refuges countrywide.)

Legal options

If you decide to take legal action against your abuser, the

following options are available under the 1981 Family Protection Act. You can go by yourself to the District Family Court in your area and take out the following orders.

Barring Order: this is given when the judge is satisfied that you are being physically abused by your spouse. It is advisable to get a solicitor and to bring any evidence or witnesses you may have to the hearing. Under a barring order, your spouse can be ordered to leave the family home for up to twelve months. If your spouse breaks the order he will be arrested and charged. You do not have to be in the family home to get the order, and your spouse does not have to be living in the home to be barred from it.

To take out a barring order you must go to your District Family Court and take out a summons for a barring order. A barring order does not come into immediate effect because you must wait for a court hearing. You and your spouse will be notified of the date.

Protection Order: a protection order comes into force immediately and gives the gardaí the right to arrest and charge the person abusing you or threatening you with violence of any kind. A protection order is granted only if you are taking out a summons for a barring order. Your spouse may remain in the family home until the court hearing for the barring order. (In many cases the existence of a protection order deters further violence.) It is advisable to inform your local gardaí that you have taken out these orders.

Custody Order: a custody order may be taken out to gain custody of your children. Access to the other parent is decided by the judge. If one parent has abused the children, supervised access may be requested. While you can take out these orders on your own and free of charge, it is always better to have legal representation, ie a solicitor, for court hearings.

The breaking of any of these orders is a criminal offence and can carry a prison sentence. Where there is sufficient evidence, your local gardaí can also charge your abuser with assault.

It is important to note that these orders can be taken out only by spouses; therefore cohabiting partners, including those in second relationships, must instead take out an injunction. This is granted by the local Circuit Court and you will require a solicitor. An injunction orders a person to stay away from you and your home. If the order is broken, your partner can be taken to court.

MAINTENANCE

In general, spouses have an obligation to support each other, and also to support their children until they reach a certain age. Unmarried people have no obligation to support each other but they are obliged to support their children.

You may, of course, make a voluntary agreement about maintenance and other aspects of separation. Any clause in such an agreement which states that you will not subsequently sue for maintenance is void. In other words, you cannot agree to waive your right to go to court to get maintenance. If you have a voluntary agreement, you may register it with the court. This means that if your ex-partner does not pay as promised, you may then use the same procedures as someone who has a maintenance order to enforce the agreement.

If you are not being maintained by your spouse, you may apply to the courts for a maintenance order under the Family Law (Maintenance of Spouses and Children) Act 1976. If you are applying for a judicial separation you would normally have all the other issues such as maintenance dealt with at the same time.

SUPPORT/INFORMATION GROUPS

The following are some of the many groups offering information, advice and/or support to separated persons and those in a subsequent relationship. Most people, especially those with children, find that these support groups are of great importance, not only because they provide a social outlet, but also because they are made up of separated or lone parents who have first-hand knowledge of how to tackle the many problems relating to marital breakdown. It should be remembered that all most of these groups are totally voluntary and therefore may shift emphasis from time to time. The details here are taken from the information given by these groups.

AIM (Family Law Information, Mediation and Counselling Centre)
32 Upper Fitzwilliam Street, Dublin 2.
(01) 661 6478
The AIM Group was set up in 1975 and offers confidential, non-directive counselling and information on family law and social welfare. They will also refer people on to the relevant helping

agencies. They provide a 24-hour telephone-answering service and will respond to letters from all parts of the country. They also have trained mediators. No appointment is necessary and the office is open from 10.00 am to 12.00 noon Monday to Friday.

Association for the Protection of the Rights of Separated Spouses
65 Meadow Mount, Dundrum, Dublin 16.
(01) 298 6855

Contact (Finglas)
St Helena's Resource Centre, Finglas Road South, Dublin
(01) 834 5407/834 3558
Contact is a voluntary organisation that offers confidential information and support to people with marital/relationship difficulties. It has developed into a pro-active organisation that seeks to address the wider issues involved in separation and the changing role of a separated person in the community.

Divorce Action Group
54 Middle Abbey Street, Dublin 1.
(01) 872 7395
DAG was set up in 1980 to campaign for the removal of the Constitutional ban on divorce. It has continued to lobby politicians for improvements in all areas of family law and, during the 1986 referendum, ran a nationwide door-to-door campaign. DAG groups in local areas tend to be partly support groups for members, but the primary aim is that of campaigning. Those interested in joining a local group should contact Head Office at the address above.

Finglas Separated Parents Group
St Helena's Resource Centre, St Helena's Rd, Finglas South, Dublin 11
(01) 834 5407
A support group for separated parents. (See also CONTACT)

Gingerbread
29 Dame Street, Dublin 2.
(01) 671 0291
Gingerbread is a self-help organisation for parents who, whether

unmarried, separated, divorced or widowed or for any other reason are obliged to bring up their child(ren) single-handed. There are branches in many parts of the country, all of which have a weekly social get-together for parents. They run family outings throughout the year, as well as annual events such as Sports Day, Hallowe'en and Christmas parties. At least one group holiday a year is organised, as well as weekend breaks and hostelling. They also operate a holiday savings scheme. Parents new to the group can attend the 'New Members' Night' held every Monday at 8.30pm in the YMCA, Aungier St, Dublin. Gingerbread gives information on social-welfare entitlements, family law, childcare and housing. There is also a counselling service to help people deal with the emotional problems that accompany separation or single parenthood. A mediation service is also offered. For information, or the addresses of local groups, contact head office at the address above.

Minus 1

c/o 83d Wellington Lane, Dublin 4
(01) 660 0256
Minus 1 groups provide support and self-help for separated parents. There are groups in Ballsbridge, Templeogue, Coolock, Clontarf and Glasnevin.

Parental Equality

Muirhevna, Dublin Road, Dundalk, Co. Louth.
(042) 33163
Set up to campaign for joint custody of children.

Parents Alone

Bunratty Drive, Coolock, Dublin 17.
(01)848 1872. Fax: (01) 848 1116
Parents Alone is a self-help group for lone parents, providing a comprehensive support and development programme for one-parent families living in the parishes of Bonnybrook, Darndale, Kilmore West and Priorswood on the north side of Dublin. The new purpose-built Centre is open Monday to Friday, 9.00 am to 5.00p.m., and offers advice and information for individuals, as well as a series of structured courses – for instance a drama programme and a money-management course – and informal

sessions for lone parents. Parents Alone provides an after-school programme for children between six and twelve, and a teenage support group. The group also arrange weekend trips and holidays for the families.

A number of similar groups are being set up in other towns. For information contact your local Citizens Advice Centre or Parents Alone at the address above.

Separated Persons Association
Carmichael House, North Brunswick Street, Dublin 7
(01) 872 0684
The Separated Persons Association is a support group and holds meetings on Mondays at 8.30p.m. in Carmichael House. These meetings are partly social, but speakers also give talks on subjects of interest such as family law. The association runs a 60s disco on Saturday nights in Gleesons on Kelly's Corner. While all are welcome at the disco, the association recommends that those interested should first attend a Monday meeting in order to meet some of the group. The association also arrranges other social events and outings for families. There is also a group in Newbridge – call the above number for details.

There are many other local groups which are useful for separated people with or without children, but which, because, of their voluntary nature, do not have phone numbers.Because of this, and because the head offices of larger organisations are lamost inevitably based in Dublin, Citizen's Advice Centres or your local TDs clinic should be contacted for details. Also, Dublin groups will be able to put you in touch with support networks in your aread.

Directory

Al-Anon (support for relatives of alcoholics): (01) 677 4195

Alcoholics Anonymous (AA):
(01) 453 8998;
Cork
(021) 500 481

Catholic Marriage Advisory Service: for list of offices nationwide call Head Office, (01) 478 0866

Childline (for children in trouble):
Freephone 1800 679 3333

Community Advice Centres (CIC)
(01 Area)
Ashbourne: Prefabs, Church Grounds, Main Street, Ashbourne, Co. Meath
(01) 835 1806
Ballymun: Library, Ballymun, Dublin 11
(01) 842 1890
Also Health Centre, Tuesday 2.30-4.30pm
Blackrock: Health Centre, Georges Ave., Blackrock, Co. Dublin
(01) 288 5406/288 2980
Blanchardstown: Roselawn Health Centre, Roselawn Rd, Blanchardstown, Dublin 15
(01) 821 2666
Bray: Health Centre, Killarney Rd, Bray, Co. Wicklow
(01) 286 0532.

Cabra West: St Finbarr's Court, Fassaugh Ave., Church of Most Precious Blood, Cabra, Dublin 7. (01) 838 1993
Clondalkin: St John's Hall, Tower Road, Clondalkin, Dublin 22
(01) 457 0861. Also Bawnogue Shopping Centre, Clondalkin
(01) 457 4043
Clontarf: 3 Church Gate Ave., Vernon Ave., Clontarf, Dublin 3.
Crumlin: 146 Sundrive Rd, Dublin 12 (01) 454 6070
Also St Vincents Centre for the Deaf: 40 Lr Drumcondra Rd, Dublin 9 (01) 830 5744
Donnycarney/Beaumont: Social Service Centre, St John's Court, Donnycarney, Dublin 9
(01) 831 9783
Dundrum: Dom Marmion House, Sandyford Rd, Dublin 16
(01) 296 0713
Dun Laoghaire: Our Lady's Clinic, Patrick St, Dun Laoghaire, Co. Dublin
(01) 280 8403, ext. 25/26
Finglas: Social Service Centre, Wellmount Rd, Dublin 11
(01) 834 2843
Greystones: Health Centre Victoria Rd, Greystones, Co. Wicklow
(01) 287 7311/287 7617
Inchicore: 52a Bulfin Rd, Inchicore, Dublin 8
(01) 453 1660

Killester: Social Service Centre, 2 Sybil Hill Rd, Dublin 5 (01) 831 3700

Liberties: 90 Meath St, Dublin 8 (01) 453 6098

Lucan: Town Hall, Lucan, Co. Dublin (01) 624 1975

Malahide: Library Car Park, Malahide, Co. Dublin (01) 845 0627

Maynooth: Main Street (above Kehoe's Delicatessen) (01) 628 5477 Also Library, Main St, Monday, Tuesday, Thursday 2.30-4.30pm, Friday 2-4pm.

Mount Argus: 179 Lr Kimmage Rd, Dublin 12 (01) 497 1225.

Palmerstown: Parish Centre, Kennelsfort Rd, Palmerstown, Dublin 20 (01) 626 0899

Rialto: Rialto Parish Centre, Old National School, Sth Circular Rd, Dublin 8 (01) 453 9965.

Skerries: Strand House Clinic, Strand Rd, Skerries, Co. Dublin (01) 849 1717

Stillorgan: St. Laurences Community Centre, Lr Kilmacud Rd, Stillorgan, Co. Dublin (01) 288 5629. Also St Theresa's Community Centre, North Ave, Mt Merrion (01) 288 8700

Swords: 10 North Street, Swords, Co. Dublin (01) 840 687

Tallaght: 1 Main St, Tallaght, Dublin 24 (01) 451 5911/451 3731

Whitehall: Social Service Centre, Collins Ave., Whitehall, Dublin 9 (01) 837 0472

OUTSIDE 01 AREA

Carlow
Carlow: St Catherines Community Centre, St Josephs Rd (0503) 31063

Kildare
Athy: Courthouse, Athy.
Newbridge: St Anne's Parish Centre, Station Rd (045) 31735

Kilkenny
Kilkenny: Desart Hall, New St (056) 62755

Laois
Abbeyleix. Main St, **Longford**
Longford: St Mels Rd (043) 41069

Louth
Ardee: c/o Day Care Centre, Church Hill (041) 53045
Drogheda: Community Services Centre. Fair St (041) 36084
Dundalk. 15a Clanbrassil St (042) 32848

Meath
Navan: Trimgate St (046) 21937.

Monaghan
Carrickmacross: c/o Credit Union, 17 O'Neill St, Carrickmacross (042) 61006/61923

Offaly
Tullamore: 18 Chapel St,
Tullamore (0506) 52204
Westmeath
Athlone: Dr Dobb's Memorial
Home, Northgate St
(0902) 72174
Mullingar: Social Service
Centre. Bishopsgate St
(044) 40700
Waterford
Dungarvan: The Courthouse.
Waterford. 37 Lr Yellow Rd.
(051) 75261

OTHER CONTACTS
**Coolock Community Law
Centre**: Northside Shopping
Centre, Dublin 5
(01) 847 7804

**Eastern Health Board
Community Welfare Service**:
Charles St, Dublin 7
(01) 872 5104.

**Eastern Health Board
Homeless Section:** Housing
Department, Civic Offices,
Fishamble St; or Corporation
Offices, Shopping Centre,
Ballymun
 (01) 679 6111

Family Mediation Service:
Block 1, Irish Life Centre, Lr
Abbey St, Dublin 1
(01) 872 8277

**Federation of Services for
Unmarried Parents and
Children:** 36 Lr Rathmines
Rd, Dublin 6 (01) 496 4155

**FISC (Free Financial Advice
Centres):** see CICs

**FLAC (Free Legal Advice
Centres):** Head Office, 49
South William St, Dublin 2
(01) 679 4239.
2 Tuckey St, Cork   MAIN .
(021) 307 969.

**Community Information
Centre,** Sackville Place,
Dublin 1. St Andrews
Resource Centre, 116 Pearse
St, Dublin 2.
(See also CICs)

Gay Switchboard: Phone
(01) 8721055 for information
on local numbers.

**INFORMATION AND
COUNSELLING**
**Irish Widowers and Deserted
Husband's Association:** 54
Foster Tce, Ballybough,
Dublin 3 (01) 855 2334

Legal Aid:
Athlone (0902) 74694
Castlebar (094) 24334
Cork (021) 273 653
Dublin (01) 878 7295
Dundalk (O42) 30448
Galway (091) 61650
Limerick (061) 314 599
Sligo (071) 61670
Tralee (066) 26900
Waterford (051) 55814

Lesbian Line:
Cork (021) 317 026;
Dublin (01) 661 3777

**Marriage Counselling
Service:** 24 Grafton St,
Dublin 2 (01) 872 0341
Rape Crisis Centres
Clonmel: 14 Wellington St
(052) 24111
Cork: 27a McCurtain St
(021) 96086
Dublin: 70 Lr Leeson St,
Dublin 2 (01) 661 4911
Galway: 3 Augustine St
(091) 64983
Kilkenny (056) 51555
Limerick: 17 Upper Mallow St
(061) 311511
Tralee: (066) 23122
Waterford: (051) 76322

**Tallaght Women's Contact
Centre:** (01) 452 4883

Women's Aid Helpline:
freephone 1800 341 900

Women's Refuges
Athlone: Auburn,
Moate Rd (0902) 74122

Bray: (01) 286 7960
Cork: Cluan Laoi,
Kyrl St
(021) 509 800.
Edel House,
14 Dyke Parade
(021) 22075
Derry: 7 London St
(0504) 263 174
Dublin:
Aoibhneas,
1 Stillogue Rd,
Ballymun
(01) 842 2377.
Women's Aid, PO Box 791,
Dublin 7
(01) 496 1002/872 3122
(administration)
(01) 453 4141
Haven House,
Dublin 7
(01) 873 2279
Galway: (091) 65985
Limerick: Adapt House,
Rosbrien (061) 42345
Navan: (046) 22393
Waterford: (051) 70367

Appendix:
Statistics

The statistics most widely quoted on divorce are those from the UK and the USA. Figures for other European countries, however, show marked differences.

RATIO OF MARRIAGES TO DIVORCES (1992 FIGURES)

Country	Marriages	Divorces	Ratio
Italy	303,785	25,997	11:1
Spain	218,121	27,224	8:1
Portugal	69,887	12,429	5:1
Greece	48,631	6,154	7:1
Denmark	32,188	12,981	3:1

The following table sets out the number of divorces per country in 1986 and in 1991.

Country	Divorces 86	Divorces 91	+/-	%
Greece	8,939	6,351	(-2,588)	-29%
Italy	16,857	27,350	(+10,493)	+62%
Portugal	8,411	10,619	(+2,208)	+26%
Spain	19,487	27,224	(+7,737)	+39%
Denmark	14,490	12,655	(-1,835)	-12%

Separations 86		Separations 91		
Ireland	37,245	55,143	(+17,898)	+48%

(*Figures*: Eurostat, and 1986 and 1991 Census)

The increase in separations in Ireland shows that we are almost at the top of the league at the moment.

Biographies

Dervla Browne

Dervla Browne was born in Clonmel, County Tipperary. She graduated from UCC in 1982 with a BCL degree. She attended UCG for two years where she did an LLB. She was called to the bar in 1986 and has practised in Dublin, mainly in the area of family law, since then. In 1989 Attic Press published her book – *Separation and Divorce Matters for Women*.

Rosheen Callender

Rosheen Callender holds a BA (Mod.) (Econ.), and is an economist in the Research Department of SIPTU (at present working as Special Adviser to the Minister for Social Welfare). She specialises in the areas of tax and social welfare reform, health and social policy, pensions, employment and equality law, and general industrial and economic policy. She has written extensively on these subjects and has published books on understanding company accounts (*Account for Yourself*, 1977) and on Irish and European equality law (*Equality in Law Between Men and Women*, 1989 and 1994).

Rosheen was an ICTU nominee to the National Pensions Board, a founder member of the Basic Income European Network and has represented Ireland on the EU's Network of Experts on the Implementation of the Equlity Directives. She is also a member of the Expert Working Group on the Integration of Tax and Social Wefare, which was set up in 1993 and is due to report in mid-1995.

Sheila Greene

After training as a clinical psychologist at the Institute of Psychiatry in London, Dr Sheila Greene worked in the Children's Hospital in Boston before joining the staff of the Psychology Department in Trinity College Dublin where she is now a senior lecturer specialising in developmental psychology and the psychology of women. Dr Greene is currently the Dean of the Faculty of Arts (Humanities) in Trinity College.

Mags O' Brien

Mags O'Brien is the Chairperson of Divorce Action Group and has held various positions in the group for the past ten years, and was active in the 1986 Referendum campaign. A mature night student, she is in her final year of a BA programme in Industrial Relations, in the National College of Industrial Relations. Mags O'Brien is a member of SIPTU, President of the NCIR Student's Union and a member of the Governing Body of the NCIR.

Finóla Ó Riagáin

Finóla Ó Riagáin holds a postgraduate Diploma in Sociology and Social Research from UCD. She is a researcher with the AIM group, and has prepared its annual statistical reports since 1989. Finóla Ó Riagáin undertakes research into the social pattern and trend of marital breakdown and separation in Ireland. She is also a counsellor and family mediator with AIM.

Patrick Riordan SJ

Patrick Riordan SJ is Dean of the faculty of philosophy, the Milltown Institute of Theology and Philosophy, Dublin. In graduate studies in philosophy at Munich and Innsbruck he specialised in the philosophy of justice. He has published a book entitled *The Practical Philosophy of Oswald Schwemmer* (University Press of America, 1991), and is the author of many articles dealing with issues of law, politics and justice. He teaches courses in political philosophy and related areas, also at the National College of Industrial Relations. He has twice been Visiting Professor at the Ateneo de Manila Universtity in the Phillipines.